The Berlioz Style

UNIVERSITY OF DURHAM

PUBLICATIONS

The Berlioz Style

BRIAN PRIMMER

LONDON
OXFORD UNIVERSITY PRESS
NEW YORK   TORONTO

Oxford University Press, Ely House, London W.1

GLASGOW NEW YORK TORONTO MELBOURNE WELLINGTON
CAPE TOWN IBADAN NAIROBI DAR ES SALAAM LUSAKA ADDIS ABABA
DELHI BOMBAY CALCUTTA MADRAS KARACHI LAHORE DACCA
KUALA LUMPUR SINGAPORE HONG KONG TOKYO

ISBN 0 19 713136 0

First published 1973
Second impression 1975

PRINTED IN GREAT BRITAIN
BY W & J MACKAY LIMITED, CHATHAM
BY PHOTO-LITHO

Contents

78532

Preface

This book is intended for students of music rather than for the general reader. It attempts to discover some of the expressive technical procedures used by Berlioz in the making of his music, and to illuminate the careful workmanship which informs and sustains his colourful musical structures. Like rhapsody and panegyric, it sprang from great musical enjoyment: and to them it should stand as complement, not substitute. If it does no more than provoke discussion it will have served its prime purpose.

Durham 1972   BRIAN PRIMMER

There is a dark
Invisible workmanship that reconciles
Discordant elements, and makes them move
In one society.

WILLIAM WORDSWORTH

[I]

Berlioz and the French Tradition

LTHOUGH BERLIOZ' MUSIC WAS BOTH PLAYED AND appreciated in the Anglo-Saxon world, and despite the fact that he many times paid tribute to the nature of the German muse, its character remains essentially French. The best of French music has always been bathed in wit and intimately concerned with mood, colour and gesture, fruits of its constant concern with the lyric stage and its perennial interest in what can best be described as spectacle. Thus, whether it be the setting of words, the accompaniment of bodily movement or the more generalized evocation of a mood suggested by a title, plastic values, the sense of poetry and the inspiration of the dance are never far away.

Savouring also the passing moment it has developed and preserved an interest in the details of melodic inflexion, harmonic piquancy and rhythmic subtlety which is less directly concerned with continuous tonal argument than is that of its German neighbours. At its worst it can be either frothy or academic, sometimes both by turn: but at its best it has a poise and *élan* which soar like the traceries of the finest Gothic cathedral. Like all essentially linear art it is enthralled by the formal and expressive possibilities of design, and pattern and the variation of pattern are integral parts of its language, vehicles of its deepest feeling and manifestations of its most glorious ideals. For this reason it is more open to exotic influences and sympathetic to Eastern minds than is the music from the further shores of the Rhine. The political agreement which France sought with Russia after the disasters of 1870 has a much more than political significance.

Generally and by intention free from ponderous moral overtones,

I

it has been able, by its emphasis upon feeling rather than message, to preserve the ancient integrity of significant design through a constant search for new arrangements and fresh, expressive *combinaisons*, a word which together with its concomitants *contrastes, oppositions* and *effets*, appears time and again in French critical writings upon music of the nineteenth century. Whilst they do not explain, these words and the overtones and implications they engender do at least indicate the nature of the gulf which separated the Gallic from the German muse and which gave to the music of each nation so very different a sound.

Whereas, even at their most Romantic, the German composers of the nineteenth century tended to be confined within the bounds of a system of musical dialectic which was increasing rapidly in density and complication, the French composers were heirs to a traditional way of thinking which, because of its pursuit of line rather than mass, was more open-ended and far-reaching: and in both directions, too. It is for this reason that Liszt rather than Wagner can be regarded as the true fore-runner of the twentieth century, and it is for this reason also that the line which runs from Rameau to Messiaen is a great deal more spectacular, subtle, piquant, colourful and elegant than is that which runs from Haydn to Richard Strauss. Perhaps the Germans were more inclined to separate what was said from the manner of its saying, to regard form and content as divisibles, to emphasize the moral rather than the aesthetic and expressive qualities of the latter, to engage in arguments rather than illuminate the field of possibilities centring upon a basic and all-pervasive *idée*. In the true sense of both words the German composers were Prophets before Poets, having about them more of the atmosphere of the Old Testament than the clear air of the Ancient World. To them the forest-depth meant more than the mountain-top, and it is not surprising that the most common accusation levelled against them by the majority of French critics, including Berlioz himself, was that of a woeful lack of *clarté*.

Everything about Berlioz' music and his critical writings bespeaks the Frenchman. His love for the Classical authors, particularly for Virgil, reflects that regard for clearness of thought and expression which is a perpetual hallmark of French intellectual activity, and which acknowledges the expressive force of suitably elegant statement. This love stayed with him all his life, culminating specifically in the magnificent pages of *Les Troyens* for which in some ways all his previous work had been but a preparation, and disseminating itself throughout his music generally in that awareness of the expressive potential of plastic line which A. W. von Schlegel maintained to be the essential characteristic of Ancient art. His critical writings, which form an essential complement to his music and which, through the typically French terms and phrases they employ, illuminate the whole cast of his artistic thinking, display similar qualities of directness, allied to a wit of which Schumann, his greatest German competitor in this field, was quite incapable. The sense of irony and satire which was so strong an element in his character is mirrored in his affection for, and frequent quotation from, the fables of La Fontaine, whilst his Memoirs stand in the tradition initiated by Rousseau and continued with varying degrees of frankness and exuberance by most French writers from Chateaubriand to Jean Genet. All Berlioz' literary and critical works evidence a professional concern for the basic stuffs of music, an impatience with pretentious theorizing about its philosophical significance and moral import, and a deep-rooted care for its expressive function and purpose. More than most, I believe, his method of composition was systematic: but unlike many he refrained from forming it into a System. His disapproving reaction to certain chords in the finale of Beethoven's Ninth Symphony, despite the fact that they anticipate in depth his own subtle technique of extended harmonic development, and his lack of sympathy for the whole procedure of the Prelude to *Tristan*: both betray that strain of academicism for which the French are at once famous and infamous in the eyes of other peoples. Berlioz himself gave voice to this deep-rooted national instinct when he stated that above all else Conservatoires ought to conserve. His belief in the exclusiveness of good music, a belief which arose from his pursuit of refined feeling and disciplined expressiveness, underlines his general distaste for the mob in all things, a distaste he shared with the *philosophes* of the preceding century as well as with many of the finer Romantic spirits of his own, and which is revealed in his somewhat equivocal attitude to the revolutions and political upheavals which shook the contemporary world. No one took a firmer stand against the Philistines. Upon no one did they turn with greater vehemence.

Berlioz' music exemplifies all the perennial touchstones of

French artistic ideals: clarity, economy, delicacy, wit, exuberance, elegance, refinement and deep feeling. And nothing in his music can be divorced from the *idée fixe* of passionate expressiveness. The expressive power of artistically disciplined sound was both the source of his work and the continuum in which it moved. It was his obsession in a world dedicated generally to the kind of obsession displayed by M. Grandet, and it was no accident that Balzac and Berlioz were fellow nationals and contemporaries. What could be clearer than the broad formal outlines of his large orchestral works or more economical than the manipulation of great masses in the *Te Deum* or *Requiem*? What music is more delicate and witty than the lighter songs with their characteristic twists of line and harmony, or more colourful and exuberant than the overture to *Benvenuto Cellini*? Who has had a more expressive touch in orchestration, or set a more disciplined hand to the control of unusual musical syntax? Technically, what is more elegant and impassioned than his command of the truly melodic line, or the manner in which poetic imagination is allowed to create and fashion the fugato and polyphonic textures which occur in almost every extended work? Where shall we find greater refinement than in the musical *effet* produced by the balance of *contraste et opposition* in the Angels' Chorus from *L'Enfance du Christ*? And in any piece of music which we might care to name, what could be done more logically or more effectively, could be aurally more satisfying or intellectually more stimulating, aesthetically more elegant or emotionally more expressive? In a phrase, what music could manifest more cogently the constant yet esoteric values of French aesthetic ideals?

How much Berlioz' music was a part of his native tradition, how deeply national rather than nationalistic it was at all times, can be seen by even a cursory glance at the scores of some of his predecessors and contemporaries. The massing of large forces in contrasting and complementary bodies, vocal and instrumental, was one of the commonest textures of the Revolutionary Period, an echo from the past analogous to that which then informed the whole structure of French society. Patriotic compositions for two, three or four choirs and orchestras were a commonplace of the time. There is nothing original in conception about the layout of Berlioz' *Te Deum, Grande Messe des Morts* or *Symphonie funèbre et triomphale*. Indeed, the opposite is the case. Since they were all destined for great national occasions what else could a truly French composer do? The originality lies in Berlioz' instinctive understanding of the problems of space and distance, in the quality of the music with which he filled and traversed them and in the *effets* he created by fresh *combinaisons* achieved by a considered and sensitively refined use of *contrastes et oppositions*. This massive tradition originates in the polychoral compositions of sixteenth-century Venice, a city with which France had always had many and varied ties. This was also the city whose canzonas and operatic sinfonias, in their own turn owing much to the contemporary taste for things *alla francese*, had stimulated the growth of the peculiarly rhythmic and contrapuntal French Overture. And if there is much in Berlioz' music that is reminiscent of the attitudes and practices we now label Baroque, the cause is to be found in the strength and continuity of this ancient practice and tradition. Massiveness of this kind brings with it its own inherent formal and stylistic qualities. Harmony tends to display a fundamental clarity, a relatively slow rate of change and a curiousness of chordal juxtapositioning which seeks expressiveness through a series of illuminating and contrasted effects rather than through a sense of continuous dialectical progress. The contrast of instrumental and vocal masses encourages the opposition of complementary timbres in all fields, and promotes the use of primary musical colours. This in its turn leads to the extension of orchestration techniques by a vital regeneration of old practices. Though it differs in kind from that demanded of composers of the dialectical school, the discipline required for the manipulation of all these interacting forces is not one whit the less; and true artistic discipline, acknowledging and working within the bounds of the chosen medium and the consciously inherited attitude, is one of the strongest elements in Berlioz' music. In a very real and significant sense it possesses the qualities of great architecture and great sculpture. These qualities were recognized as essential ingredients of the French style by such a man as Balzac when he used what was primarily a jewelling term, *sertisseur,* to describe Meyerbeer's compositional procedures in *Robert le diable*. In a more general sense they were implied also by Théophile Gautier when he professed himself to be a man for whom the visible world existed. Thus there is a genuine feeling for the past, for the present worth of ancient values 'and ideals within the very fabric of Berlioz' music which makes it in this sense, perhaps, more truly Romantic and timeless than that of any other composer of the age.

In matters of audacious orchestral usage and effect Berlioz had been anticipated by F. J. Gossec who, in the 1760s, produced a *Messe des morts* which, in the *Tuba mirum* section, banished the woodwind to a distance whilst keeping the strings close to hand. Moreover, these strings were directed to play *pianissimo* and *tremolando* in the upper registers. This same composer wrote an oratorio, *La Nativité*, in which a chorus of Angels was directed to sing from an invisible and distant platform, an effect remarkably prophetic of the analogous chorus in *L'Enfance du Christ,* and in line with thousands of other operatic and orchestral works of the period. By the time of Meyerbeer's maturity, off-stage choirs and orchestras and effects *da lontano* had become almost a *sine qua non* of the French lyric stage. This is the spectacular made audible, sounding perspective, aural geometry, the outcome of a national emphasis upon Opera which perceived the poetry within Reason and the immanent passion of control.

Another French composer of the time, famous for his startling orchestral colours and modulatory turns, was Étienne Méhul. Méhul was much admired by Beethoven, who learned a great deal about instrumental effects and orchestral layout—especially those connected with timpani parts, melodic bass-lines and off-stage trumpet calls—from the deep study he gave to his operas and symphonic works. It is possible that the original inspiration for the extremely popular *allegretto* in Beethoven's Seventh Symphony —in its turn a fore-runner of the *Marche des Pèlerins* in *Harold en Italie,* and the *Prière* from *Benvenuto Cellini*—came from the corresponding movement in the D major symphony by Méhul.

Even that old *perruque* Grétry had had some remarkable ideas on the possible future development of orchestral music, of which he writes in his Memoirs and which point the way to the expressive, dramatic and illustrative possibilities of the medium. His love for Shakespeare's works, his belief in the artistic worth of genuine melodrama, his interest in the effects of hidden orchestras and the composition of music for huge public places and occasions, together with his concern for music's place in elementary education (a point to be enlarged upon by Berlioz himself throughout his career) bespeak an attitude which, whilst remaining for him largely theoretical, was stimulating and provocative to his more gifted contemporaries and successors.

Jean Francois Lesueur, Berlioz' revered master and friend for many years, had aimed at creating a 'dramatic and descriptive' sacred music during his period as Maître at Nôtre Dame de Paris. This aim has a significantly Berliozian ring, especially if we substitute the word 'expressive' for Lesueur's own choice of 'descriptive', as does his demand for what Barzun has termed 'corps of trombones and salvos of musketry' in the music he wrote for the coronation of Napoleon I. Some of Lesueur's harmonic, tonal and rhythmic procedures foretell those of his most famous pupil, albeit a little weakly. In the peroration to the final chorus which serves both his first and third *Te Deum* for instance, the following passage occurs.

Later, in his own music, and following the example of Gluck, Lesueur and the whole company of operatically-motivated composers, Berlioz was to make much of the expressive and dramatic possibilities of successions of diminished seventh chords, imbuing what was so often in lesser hands no more than a vulgar cliché with the passionate integrity of his own emotional experience.

More interesting to us, however, particularly in view of such movements as the *Marche des Pèlerins* in *Harold en Italie* or the *Prière* in *Benvenuto Cellini,* are the following varied cadential passages from a section of Lesueur's *Premier Te Deum*. It is an excellent example of the possible *effet* of different linear twists and harmonic-cum-tonal *combinaisons*. In itself it may not be very successful. But how stimulating such variations of the cadential pattern must have been to Berlioz. Such is the kind of offering which talent makes to genius and by which genius alone can profit.

(a)

The banality of conventional Italian-type codas was one of Berlioz' particular *bêtes-noires*. Not even Beethoven could escape

his strictures in this respect, as his remarks upon the closing bars of
the second movement of the Eighth Symphony clearly show. This
banality Berlioz himself tried always to avoid, at times with somewhat wayward results but more often with success. He never
achieved that kind of alternative banality to which analogous
opportunities so often prompted Meyerbeer.

Another older contemporary and teacher of Berlioz was Anto-
nin Reicha, friend and one-time orchestral colleague of Beethoven
at Bonn, writer of chords for the timpani in his *Harmonie des
Sphères,* and composer of some of the most peculiar and, to my
mind at least, unsuccessful fugues which have ever been penned.
Reicha's taste for fugal expositions in which each successive entry
was pitched in the key a third higher or lower than the preceding
one played havoc with the accepted rules of fugal writing, as did
his occasional sudden *caesurae* and dramatically inflamed cadenzas. It
is intriguing to picture Cherubini's reaction upon finding himself
one of the dedicatees of the set of twelve fugues for the piano
which Reicha published in 1799. The tonal and textural chaos
which resulted from this practice produced very bad pieces of
music; but the ideas enshrined within them, together with the
example afforded by the similar tonal juxtapositionings in the recitative passages of lyric tragedy and serious opera, which also
sought an extension of dramatic expressiveness by this means,
must have encouraged his *avant-garde* contemporaries to question
the desirability of continuing to use none but the old methods in
newly-composed and differently motivated structures. Certainly it
created a new attitude towards the expressive possibilities of in-
stant key change and apposition, an attitude which both grew
from, and flourished in, the aesthetic basis of the French tradition.
According to Berlioz, Reicha gave very good counterpoint lessons
at the Conservatoire. But whatever the value of these to the general
run of music students, the oddity of much of the music he wrote
outside of the classroom must surely have been of more interest to
Berlioz himself. The following quotation from the third fugue of
this set is a good example of the general style.

Fugue 3

10

Even Cherubini, a master of musical notes if ever there was one, preserved a peculiarly French attitude in his approach to the drama, operatic or liturgical. This attitude can be traced in the contours of many of his vocal lines as well as in the often sombre but expressively apt orchestration which he employs. The vocal contours are directly descended from, and reminiscent of, those of Rameau, whilst the dramatic conception and the manner of its orchestration owe a great deal to Gluck.

Berlioz' music shows itself to be a part of this remarkable tradition in many ways. His persistent interest in the musical and expressive possibilities of rhythm is such a case. Marked rhythmic figurations had been an integral feature of French music since the days of the rhythmic modes, whilst in the seventeenth and eighteenth centuries the double-dottings and the *notes inégales* were essential traits of the French style. It was in the field of rhythmic inventiveness that Berlioz considered contemporary music to be at its most unadventurous; and his interest in, and arrangements of, complex rhythmic patterns produced some of the most attractive, arresting and expressive pages in his work. In this direction also he may have received some specific stimulation from Reicha, whose *L'Art du Varier* (1802–4) explored the possibilities of rhythmic, metrical and tempo contrasts, as well as those of harmonic and textural development, in a set of very intriguing keyboard variations. Nor was the set of twelve piano fugues previously mentioned without its metrical experiments, as the second of the following examples shows.

(a)
Variation 5 (L'Art du Varier)

(b)
Fugue 7 Mesure composée (Douze fugues)

Other instances of Berlioz' natural place in this tradition can be heard in the popular, and one might say almost Republican, atmosphere of works such as the *Symphonie funèbre et triomphale*. The use of large, complementary musical forces for more rarified ends is seen in the *Te Deum* or, at its most lucid and witty, in *Sara la Baigneuse*. Effects *da lontano*—effects rehallowed to Romantic musical usage as much by the comments of Senancour's *Obermann* as by any specifically musical example—are frequent, the best known being those in the third movement of the *Symphonie fantastique*, the last movement of *Harold en Italie* and the Angels' Chorus from *L'Enfance du Christ*. His use of timpani chords or note clusters in the *Symphonie fantastique* continues that poetic and expressive practice initiated by Reicha in the *Harmonie des sphères* and continued by Beethoven in his Ninth Symphony. Reicha's practices with tertial tonal relationships in instrumental music, as well as those indulged by all composers of serious operatic recitative, take a similar path of development, employed by Beethoven and many others at the time, but becoming one of Berlioz' most common tonal procedures.

Rameau's most characteristic vocal cadence

is used by both Cherubini and Berlioz and can still be heard in the operas of later French composers such as Gounod and Saint-Saëns, whilst the appoggiatura which rounds off so many of Berlioz' melodic phrases is a commonplace of French music, deriving ultimately from the peculiarities of its prosody when sung. The characteristic harmony supporting these melodic sighs—generally an augmented or perfect fourth resolving on to a third, the former having a national flavour all of its own—is as common a feature of Lesueur's music as it is of that of Berlioz.

A detailed study of Berlioz' tonal syntax and harmonic grammar will be undertaken in the chapters to come. It is enough to say at the moment that his overriding concern for the expressive powers of music, and his typically Gallic taste for varieties of illuminating *combinaisons*, led him to use conventional harmonies in ways which did not at all obey the obvious dictates of long-range tonal argument. The outlines of his structures may coincide with the basic minimum demands of this procedure—beginning and ending in the same key for instance, or making a move to the conventional dominant area at roughly the 'right' place and time—but what happens within these outlines is the product of another set of values. His procedures are always logical; he would not have been French if they had been otherwise. But it is the logic of expressiveness, the poetry of the moment and the medium rather than that of consistent and sustained tonal dialectic. Seeking *effet* through new *combinaisons* and by means of fresh *contrastes et oppositions*, he was able to illuminate rather than discuss expressive musical hypotheses, and thereby to replace possible tendentiousness with certain wit. It is precisely here that so many criticisms of his work go astray. Being nurtured upon instrumental rather than operatic values, upon mass rather than line, content before form, they confuse musical expressiveness with verbal meaning, seeing literary programmes as the only possible explanations for grammatical peculiarities which they insist upon regarding as syntactical aberrations. Hence there has grown up a legend about Berlioz' technical incompetence and programmatic musical behaviour which can be justified only so long as his music is heard from this mistaken point of view. It is a Teutonic rather than a Gallic point of view, as every French critic was prepared to say in the earlier days of the nineteenth century, though mostly in reference to music by composers other than Berlioz.

It is also commonly assumed that the Romantic composers were great inventors of new chords. This is not so. As Professor Butterfield has pointed out in his *Origins of Modern Science*, it is not so much the discovery of new facts as the rearrangement of known facts within a new framework of reference which re-creates the world and stimulates fresh answers to old and perennial problems. Perhaps this is why the French tradition, with its insistence upon the art of arrangement and rearrangement in all intellectual, critical and artistic activity, has preferred ethics to morals, realized the true power of irony and wit and frequently set the outside world by the ears. And perhaps also this is why the French tradition, with its love of *effet* created through ever-changing *combinaisons* formed from a constant flow of differing *contrastes et oppositions*, has retained its strong Classical flavour. It has never lost sight of either the elegance or the passion beneath the surface of a disciplined antithesis and balance. No western European nation has so taken to heart da Vinci's aphorism that Art is born of constraint. For the French tradition to become Romantic, therefore, it needed not the ideal of total freedom beyond the bounds of all restraint, but the much more demanding call of an appropriately ordered and deeply felt liberty. In the music of Berlioz it achieved just this, a revolution without a rebellion.

Whatever may be the truth of these reflections in general, they have undoubted relevance to Berlioz and to his music. This open-ended attitude, in which the individuality lies in the construction and not in the vocabulary, is typical of the procedures adopted by French composers in general. Reicha's fugues contain nothing new in the way of harmonies, but their grammar is astonishing. Méhul's extant symphonies similarly reveal curiosities of grammatical construction which do not require the spiciness of a strange vocabulary to make their startling effect. The list of examples could be prolonged almost indefinitely. But an examination of the scores by Berlioz' predecessors, contemporaries and successors, as well as a study of those by Berlioz himself, shows that the true French tradition was, and continued to be, an esoteric and, in the most passionate sense of the word, a geometrical one. Berlioz is a solitary figure not because he stands outside of this tradition but because he stands at its head.

[2]

Berlioz and Melody

T HE MOST NOTICEABLE FEATURES OF BERLIOZ' MELO-
dies are their length, their comprehensiveness, their subtlety,
their frequent waywardness and their generally deep expressive power. Their length is often extreme when compared with
that of melodies by other composers and always unusual—save
when the particular expressive intention demands otherwise, as in
the case of the *idée fixe* from *Harold en Italie*. Essentially they are
examples of melodic prose rather than instances of tuneful verse:
and in an age devoted primarily to the cultivation and sensual
enjoyment of the latter they were bound both to be noticed and
to be commented upon. It is not surprising, therefore, that in his
own day the very existence of melody in Berlioz' works should
have been questioned by many, and that this question should have
become a central thread in the so-called Berlioz problem. The
irregularity of their internal phrasing gives them a comprehensiveness of technical detail and emotional colouring analogous to that
found in a Shakespeare scene and is in some ways reminiscent of
Baroque melodic styles. This is significant, for it was not only in
his large-scale open forms that Berlioz was inspired by Shakespeare
but also in the details of his structures, in the infinite variety of his
phrase-shapings and their attendant emotional colouring. This
made it possible for him to create a typically Romantic *mélange*, to
fuse many seemingly contradictory elements into one complex but
unified whole. Speaking in a diatonic, mixed or even wholly
chromatic language these melodic lines reflect and outline that
extension of tonal and grammatical construction which was
Berlioz' peculiar contribution to Romantic music and which is
responsible for the noticeable individuality of his own music's
sound. This matter of the grammar of music brings us to the heart
of the problem which his works still pose to the general listener as

well as to the critic. It is a fact of aural experience that however deeply it may have been infused with chromaticism and modal ambiguity, Berlioz' musical language remains at heart traditional and, in its operatically-inspired harmonic vocabulary, even somewhat old-fashioned. It is not the individual chords which require new technical descriptions but the way in which they are put together. He never rode with Liszt in the *Lugubrious Gondola*, nor trod the thorny path of the *Via Crucis*. The undeniable sense of discomfort and unease which, on first acquaintance, seems to inform certain passages and movements in his work is due to the very real tension which existed between the pull of his creative imagination and the restrictions of the tonal system through which it had to work. Like all of us he was a child of his time, and more than most of us was he a true son of his native land. Wishing to be understood, therefore, he used the language natural to both. If he had been born fifty years later things might have been different: and it might be argued that the fundamental personal tragedy in his far from easy life was the fact that he was born a Frenchman in 1803. This much however is certain: his native respect for intelligence and clear thinking—a respect made manifest in his critical writings upon the works of others as well as in the music he composed himself—made him a revolutionary figure rather than a rebellious one, a reformer and not a destroyer. Although he recharged the grammatical possibilities of musical structure almost beyond belief, he never attempted to overthrow the fundamental rule of tonality. He preferred to regroup rather than to overturn. This was (and is yet) an essentially French reaction to the Romantic challenge: and the difference between early Romanticism in France and that in Germany—a difference of date as well as one of style and inheritance—is pointed by the Gallic tendency to replace the ideas of the *ancien régime* with the ideals of the *ancient world*. Frenchman espoused the idea of Glory longer than did the inhabitants of any other European nation, and this basically Ancient and then Renaissance ideal was reflected in their definitions of Beauty as much as in their attempts at military domination. Nothing expresses this more succinctly than the transformation, in the texts of so many public songs and choruses of the Revolutionary Period and beyond, of the word *romantique* into the rallying call *Rome Antique*. In this single play upon words the unique flavour of the traditional French attitude is crystallized. Its effect upon composers born into or working through the early years of the nineteenth century was profound.

In Berlioz' music the conventional nature of the main tonal shifts in all his extended 'sonata' form movements and works is absolute. In the last analysis also his melodies tend to rest upon a plain, diatonic framework made up of step and triad, whatever degree of expressive chromaticism may colour them. Thus, however lengthy, they remain set pieces *sui generis*: and, although their punctuation may be unusual, it is rarely wholly ambiguous. It is true that more than those by any other composer of the time Berlioz' lines were truly melodic. But this truth is relative to the contemporary situation and not absolute. His methods of melodic construction were akin to those of the original makers of Gregorian chant, an assertion which should make increasing sense as we examine the lineaments of his individual lines and discover to what extent they appear to depend upon the manipulation of expressive formulae. But his accent was that of nineteenth-century France, an accent modified by the traditional concepts of harmony and ultimately conditioned by the accepted conventions of European tonality. Melody lies at the centre of his art, inspiring harmonic progressions, maintaining polyphonic textures and giving rise to many sonorous felicities never previously heard. This centrality of melody is perhaps the most important single factor in his music.. Nevertheless, it remains bounded by the tonal system inherited from Beethoven, a situation symbolic of the clash between logic and prophecy which was the catalytic force in the creation of all his works and in the formation of his peculiar and inimitable musical style.

The pages that follow are devoted to an analysis of some of Berlioz' most characteristic or well-known melodies. There is no perfect and unchallengeable system of melodic analysis, and I claim for these pages no more than a hearing. A possible point of view is enshrined within them. And although I hope it is not entirely unenlightening I make no claim whatsoever for its exclusive truthfulness. All music critics and academic analysts would do well to recall F. L. Lucas's sage remark that criticism becomes charlatanism only when the critic deludes himself into thinking that *his* word is *the* word, and that that is the *last* word.

FANTASTIC SYMPHONY: IDÉE FIXE

Since this is perhaps Berlioz' best-known melody it seems fitting
that our investigations should begin with it.

Of forty bars duration (tempo and stylistic direction *Allegro
agitato e appassionato assai*), it contains eight phrases in a bar ratio-
pattern to one another of 8:7:4:4:4:5:2:6. These are set within
an over-all lemniscate curve which achieves its climax in bar twenty-
eight. Because of its predominantly rising contour, the tune has a
striving, upward-reaching quality which perfectly reflects the
emotional condition of its supposed hero/heroine. This much is
fairly obvious. The real subtlety of workmanship and feeling however is to be found in the phrasing, in the irregular lengths of its
members, the variety of their contours and the variations in their

scope. It is here, in its details of rise and fall, extension and contraction, shallowness and depth that the most intimate connection between music and expressiveness resides. And it is in this field that Berlioz' technique of formula-manipulation achieved its most subtle and artistic expression.

The bar ratio-pattern displays a principle of rhythmic construction—longer values : shorter values : longer values—characteristic of Berlioz' music. It is a principle which he assumed from the music of both Lesueur and Beethoven, respectively his teacher and his inspiration. Nothing could better reflect that sense of the eternal ebb and flow of things which lies at the heart of so much Romantic art. This feeling is supported by the tonal implications of the melody which moves from C to dD to e and back to C once more, whilst the general *élan* of the whole is due to the fact that each phrase begins with an upbeat.

In the matter of contour the first and last phrases are roughly symmetrical in design: the second is a reflection in miniature of the over-all contour: the third, fourth, fifth and sixth are lemniscates with early climactic points, a reversal of the over-all shape: whilst the seventh is a direct fall through the interval of a minor seventh. In all these phrases there is much emphasis upon continuous falling lines, some being formed from little else, which emphasis is contrary to the upward movement of the over-all melodic design. Thus there is an inherent conflict of general direction and detailed phrase-shape which creates a musical tension of strong expressive power. Inwardly it is in a state of constant flux, however purposeful its outward step may seem to be.

This is underlaid with a contrast of leaps and steps, both within and between the individual phrases. Phrases one, two, seven and eight all contain leaps—upward in the first two, downward in the last—whilst the four inner phrases are wholly continuous. The natural balance, indeed symmetry, of this plan is obvious. What is less obvious perhaps, is the expressive quality of the intervals concerned and of the contrasts between them.

In the first phrase a fourth is followed by a sixth, the whole being bounded by the interval of a seventh. In the second phrase the same initial intervals, though differently pitched, are followed by a fifth and a third, and the over-all scope of the phrase is extended to an eleventh. Thus we can see how, by doubling the number of leaps, increasing the over-all width of the phrase whilst simultaneously decreasing its length, and by involving dominant feeling as well as that of the tonic, the assertive and venturesome quality of the second phrase becomes greater than that of the first. Moreover, narrowing the tread of the second pair of intervals in phrase two gives it a certain attractive hesitancy, a growing irresolution in keeping with the over-all musical and emotional situation.

The inner phrases (3–6 inclusive) altogether dispense with leaps. Their narrow scope of a fourth, their continuity of line, their comparative shortness and the upward movement of the successive climaxes, all push us somewhat breathlessly towards the melody's ultimate aim which is top *C* in phrase six. The subtle change from *A♭* to *A♮* in phrases three and four, plus the quick tonal progression from *C* through *dD* to *e*, give added impetus to its climb and make its resolution in the last two phrases satisfying in every way.

These two concluding phrases open with wide and unhampered falls, the first of a seventh and the second of a sixth, a diminution of interval which balances the augmentation present in the two opening phrases. The last phrase, essentially a symmetrical and continuous curve, contains a fall of a major sixth, immediately offset by a rise of a minor sixth. This restores its balance and helps to relax the tension of the whole melody.

Examination of the melody in this fashion reveals not only its technical construction and expressive inclination but also the intimate relationship between them. This is the point from which Berlioz set out to discover the *genre instrumental expressif*. Accepting the age-old analogy felt to exist between linear direction and expressive intention he created from it a detailed melodic syntax, a body of shapely formulae which was capable of almost infinite refinement and adjustment. Any expressive situation, simple or complex, contemporary or ancient, popular or esoteric could be symbolized in melodic lines which, whilst yielding none of their musical autonomy to literary ideas or philosophic concepts, were nevertheless entirely conditioned by feeling. Music remained supreme: but in doing so it became wholly expressive. Although the *idée fixe* in the *Symphonie fantastique* finally achieves its aim, the path it takes is neither direct nor simple. Only one phrase, the seventh, suffers no diversion of itself, and it is significant that this phrase occurs after the climactic point of the whole line has been reached. So, through wholly musical means, the deep-seated but hesitant yearning of the Romantic sensibility was reflected in the structure of a single melody by one of its most sensitive, literate and sophisticated composers.

It is worth remarking here perhaps, how little the composition of these forty bars has taxed Berlioz' powers of true musical invention, for much of the theme consists of plain repetition and sequence. This is a characteristic of many of his lines, and in most cases the melodic extension it generates provides him with opportunities to vary and develop the tonal, harmonic or rhythmic character of their accompaniments. This last is one of his most significant and powerful expressive practices, one to which he may have been spurred by the examples of Beethoven and Reicha and one which modified his melodic invention as much as it stimulated his harmonic imagination. As we shall see in a later chapter, harmonic rather than thematic development was the essential ingredient in many of Berlioz' extended structures, and this allowed him to repeat melodic phrases both literally and sequentially without ever losing the necessary sense of organic progression and over-all musical evolution. It also enabled him to present melodies freed from the encumbrances of continuous accompaniment, especially at the outset of a movement or passage. Much of the criticism to which such lines have been subjected in the past has been due to a general failure to appreciate their function as the basic elements of harmonic evolution. From this initial failure may other misunderstandings have flowed.

With much of Berlioz' melodic writing therefore, the interest is concentrated not upon the line itself but upon the deepening relationship which develops between it and its varied accompaniments. These last may emphasize tonal or harmonic change, rhythmic contrast and development, changing orchestral colour and variety of texture or any admixture of the five. In the particular case now under discussion the interest is primarily rhythmic which, because of Berlioz' innate understanding of the problems of musical space and spacing, includes the subtlest apposition of activity and rest. In a very real way his sensitivity to the expressive possibilities of musical rhythm reopened a dimension in the art of counterpoint which had been closed for several centuries: and in many of his works all the basic elements of music itself become involved in the contrapuntal web.

Closely paralleling both the over-all contour and the individual phrase-shapes of the *idée fixe* are the variations in dynamic intensity which inform it. These, together with their variety of attendant tempo and stylistic changes—*espressivo*: *dolce*: *animando*—leave no doubt at all about the expressive intentions of the theme. This certainty about the composer's expressive intentions was one of the great practical benefits which Berlioz conferred upon French music of the period. Previously, French composers had filled their scores and parts with verbal directions and suggestions, poetic as well as practical in intention, hoping that these would increase the chances of fully sensitive and expressive performances of their music. Berlioz showed this to be unnecessary. All his markings are musical or technical, and every one of them is essential. Comments and suggestions of a wider nature were made into Prefaces or Programmes such as those associated with *Roméo et Juliette*, or with the *Symphonie fantastique*. In this, as in so many other ways, he helped to restore the purity of French music, making it unnecessary for future composers to explain their expressive intentions by word of mouth as Lesueur had expounded his to the young Berlioz on so many Sunday mornings in the past.

ROMÉO ET JULIETTE: ROMÉO SEUL

This magnificent example of an expressive musical line has given rise to more misunderstanding than almost any other in the whole body of Berlioz' *oeuvre*. Much has been written about its supposed atonality: it has even been advanced as an example of a genuine tone-row. But however interesting such theories may be, I am not myself convinced by them and certainly not when listening to the music in performance. Despite its essential chromaticism it sounds completely tonal, and its movement from tonic to dominant and back again via the chords of E and a is thoroughly in accord with the conventions of nineteenth-century tonality and harmony. Like all of Berlioz' tonal shifts this represents no more than a quantitative advance upon those of Beethoven, a subject which will more fully occupy our attention in another chapter. As the following analysis will show it is a severely disciplined line, exhibiting several features which, paradoxically, are more characteristic of the traditional 'set-piece' tune than they are of free and prose-like melody.

Encompassing twenty-one bars, its seven phrases possess a bar ratio-pattern of 2:2:4:2:2:4:4. Its highest point occurs in bar seven, one third of the way through its length, and this creates an early-climax lemniscate contour ideal for expressing deeply introverted emotions. The over-all range is a twelfth, whilst every phrase but the third, which is symmetrical, shows a contour similar to that of the whole line. Thus there is not the same degree of inherent tension between the individual phrase-shapes and the over-all contour of the melody, nor yet the same variety of design amongst the phrases themselves, as existed in the *fantastique* theme. However many falling lines there were in the *idée fixe*, its general direction was upwards. It had an over-all assertive and venturesome quality. This line on the other hand, by the nature of its phrase designs and their associated emotional implications, is intensely introverted. It probes deep rather than pushes outwards. With the exception of the third every phrase points downwards, as does the longer limb of the over-all contour. The scope of each phrase is limited, exceeding a seventh only in phrase three, and expressed mainly through continuous chromatic lines. Where leaps do occur a very careful balance between upward and downward direction is preserved. All but two of the phrases begin on a down-beat, though a certain ambivalence of stress is created by the syncopated figure with which they open ($\natural\ \natural\ \natural$), and which may be described as

23

a pseudo-upbeat. Here much depends upon the rhythmic sensitivity of the performance. The chromatic richness of this line is rigidly disciplined by the severity of its bar ratio-pattern, the squareness of its rhythmic design and the subtle melodic variation which is played upon the first two phrases by the last phrase. Like harmonic development, melodic variation is one of Berlioz's most fascinating and expressive musical characteristics. Difficult to pin down exactly in many cases, it is a constant aural experience during performances of his music and one of its most potent cohesive forces, both short-term and long-range. Closely associated with harmonic development, it underlines the essentially decorative or stylized nature of his art.

Less obviously repetitious than the *fantastique* theme, the violin line from *Roméo seul* draws its inspiration from within itself through melodic variation and rhythmic reflection, signs of a truly melodic composer. It is a great deal more severe than the *idée fixe* and, rather remarkably, a great deal more intense. I say 're-markably' only in respect of other composers, since it is one of the central traits in Berlioz' music that the more intense he becomes emotionally the greater is the discipline he exerts. It is for this reason that he is never sentimental: and it is for this reason also that he has often been accused of heartlessness. It is interesting to recall his remark that it was not so much *ma musique* that concerned him as *la musique*. This curious detachment from his own works was in many ways his musical salvation, making it possible for him to be an intermediary between Heaven and earth or between Government and People in his religious or nationally-commissioned works. However frequently other composers might proclaim their priestly *status* in that veneration of Art so characteristic of the Romantic attitude, only Hector Berlioz fulfilled a truly priestly *function*. Although this set him apart from the general run of his fellows, it gave him an isolation of which he was both conscious and proud. Few composers have been more keenly aware of their own natural artistic aristocracy: in this awareness he became a truly Byronic figure.

The extent of the expressive power which this detachment and discipline conferred upon his music is to be found in that most underrated work the *Symphonie funèbre et triomphale*, and to a consideration of the two main themes in its first movement we shall now turn.

SYMPHONIE FUNÈBRE ET TRIOMPHALE:
FIRST MOVEMENT

This work is a Berliozian version of the conventional French Republican and patriotic style, a style which appears in the oddest places in French music—in the *Offertorium* of Cherubini's *Requiem in c minor* for instance—and which is characterized as much by the timbre of its orchestration as by its national rhythmic and harmonic traits. It forms a natural link with the musical language of *Les Troyens*, the *Prélude* to the second part of which will be discussed later.

The first theme is nineteen bars long, with an over-all late-climax lemniscate contour which rises to its highest point in bar seventeen. The phrasing is complex, and strange in its 2:2:2:4:9 bar ratio-pattern. No doubt the last nine bars could be subdivided; but taken as a unit they are so excellent an example of Berlioz' *fortspinnung* technique that it seems unreal to do so.

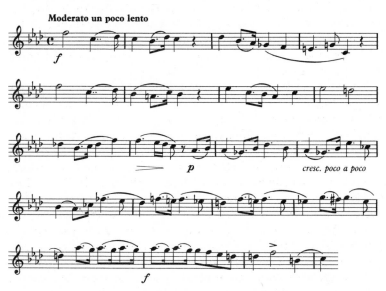

Beginning on a down-beat which emphasizes the squareness of their cut, a quality underlined also by the single and double-dotted rhythmic figures they contain, the first two phrases fall, one through a fourth and the other through a minor ninth. The third phrase begins on the same note as the first, which necessitates a wide leap between the phrases, but it moves through a fifth instead of a fourth, whilst the fourth phrase (twice the length of the preceding three) has an over-all scope of a sixth. The subtlety of linear detail here is typical of Berlioz' sense of melodic equilibrium and is impossible to express succinctly in words. Notice how

is offset by

which balance of direction and design gives the phrase a hovering quality, perfectly positioned before the final phrase.

This last, self-extending nine-bar phrase climbs slowly upwards in the manner of the *fantastique* theme, closing with a short cadenza figure which comes to rest on the dominant. This 'open end' leads to a complete repetition of the whole pattern, which this time finishes in the tonic.

The second theme, in the conventional key of the relative major $A\flat$, is thirty bars long and contains eleven phrases which fall into a bar ratio-pattern of 4:2:2:5:1:1:4:3:2:2:2:3. It achieves its highest point in bar fifteen, thus tracing a roughly symmetrical contour. For such a long theme the over-all range of an eleventh is somewhat restricted. This tells us something about Berlioz' line-drawing, especially in the so-called 'Republican' style. With all its twists, turns and chromatic inflexions it can achieve great expressive intensity over long periods without ranging across excessively wide distances. Once more its expressive and musical strength is drawn from within itself, the sign of a truly melodic composer. This accounts for the slight ambiguity of phrasing encountered in his *fortspinnung* lines and the part played in them by organic decoration.

There are some interesting melodic and rhythmic similarities between this theme and its predecessor—compare the first and the seventh phrases in the first theme with the second and the fourth phrases in this, for instance—which may or may not give support to the theories of Rudolf Reti, but which undoubtedly help the movement to cohere.

Comparison of the individual phrase-shapes in both tunes also reveals some significant features which have important expressive implications, and not for this work alone. Both themes are *funèbre*, though the minor mode of the first gives it a greater intensity, which is enhanced by the falling lines of its first three phrases. In the second theme, however, the falling lines of the second and third phrases are preceded by an almost perfectly balanced contour which rises and falls in roughly equal proportion. This, plus the expressive quality of the relative major mode in which it is pitched, gives the second theme a less deeply tragic aspect, though it remains far from gay. There is a kind of cool restraint about this statement of national grief which arises from the pattern of the notes themselves and from the impassioned technique which orders them. In both tunes there is a phrase which hovers around a central point, making it the emotional crux of the line as well as its musical turning-point. At this stage the composer has a choice. Either he can accentuate the particular expressive character established so far by continuing in the general direction already taken, or else he can balance both melody and emotion by moving along the opposite path. For Berlioz there was no real doubt. Above all things he valued musical balance—which he was never so naïve as to confuse with melodic symmetry—and, in his best works at least, emotional restraint. Thus the concluding phrase of the first theme is assertive, venturesome in the manner of the *fantastique's idée fixe*, tracing a late-climax lemniscate arc which prevents the sentiment of the whole from becoming maudlin. In the second theme, however—a major mode melody which, by its symmetrically contoured opening phrase, established immediately a feeling of grief nobly accepted —the fourth and fifth phrases move upwards, whilst the sixth has an early-climax lemniscate curve accentuating its tragic aspect, a tendency continued in the wholly descending lines of phrases eight and nine, slightly retarded by the more balanced contour of the tenth, and wholly offset by the symmetrical outline of the last. This final phrase re-establishes the emotional and musical equilibrium initiated by the first. In no other two single themes, or pair of themes, is Berlioz' manipulation of linear formulae for expressive ends so clearly demonstrated: and nowhere shall we find a better example of his innate scorn for that vulgar doctrine which sees music as the vehicle of self-expression rather than a means of artistic communication.

As for the musical language in which all this is expressed, both these tunes are good examples of the effect which his tonal thinking could have upon his melodic construction. The whole of the second part of the first theme is modulatory, its aim being the dominant minor chord with which it ends. From bar ten onwards the modulatory process takes us, however transiently, through the keys of $G\flat$, $C\flat$, $F\flat$, $D\flat$, and $E\flat$ majors and c minor, whilst its own second half turns most effectively towards the flattened supertonic ($B\flat\flat$) before concluding firmly in the tonic key. It is significant that tonal exploration and melodic *fortspinnung* should go hand in hand, one stimulating the other and demanding constant musical invention. Berlioz' melodies are at their most inventive when they are employing this ancient device.

The accompaniments to both these melodies are continuous, though of a very different character from one another. In the first ten bars of the opening theme the side-drums have a persistent rhythmic figure of a decidedly military cut, which is answered each time by a rhythm of similar character on the horns, trumpets and cornets. Together they create the composite two-bar pattern

The care with which Berlioz has indicated the dynamic variation of the side-drum part is both characteristic and significant. Every mark in a Berlioz score is meaningful, just as every one of his rhythmic patterns and instrumental dispositions is musically expressive. Thereafter, a more supple texture involving a good deal of syncopation moves above persistent crotchet beats on the side-drums, which crescendo to a climax nine bars later. It is worth noticing that the more supple texture and rhythm of the accompaniment in this passage coincides with the *fortspinnung* of the melodic line and its allied tendency to be tonally adventurous.

The second theme opens above a rippling accompaniment which is maintained until the melodic climax in bar fifteen. Then, for three bars and a half, the rhythmic pattern is more broadly designed, expressing itself in minims and crotchets, a characteristic change of momentum. The last twelve bars of the theme have constant quaver movement in some or other of the accompanying parts for eight bars, which then broaden into crotchets. The really interesting thing about this accompaniment, however, is the subtlety of harmonic alteration which underlines the small melodic variations of the first section,

and also the straight repetitions of the last.

Thus, in these two themes, all Berlioz' characteristic melodic and accompanying procedures are displayed—straightforward repetition, manipulation of linear formulae, melodic *fortspinnung*, harmonic change and tonal variety.

Just as Berlioz' melodies can speak with every kind of musical accent from the diatonic to the chromatic, so may their structures vary in length and internal arrangement from the highly individual to the merely conventional. With an artist of Berlioz' calibre however, surface convention is rarely what it seems, and never the result of thoughtlessness. If a tune appears conventional there is bound to be some good expressive-cum-musical reason for its apparent lack of individuality. In this connection, therefore, it will be instructive to examine some of his shorter or seemingly less original tunes.

HAROLD EN ITALIE: IDÉE FIXE

In itself the Harold theme seems to have nothing in particular to recommend it. Lacking initial upbeats and never moving away from the tonic key, its eight bars fall into two equal and balanced phrases beneath a late-climax lemniscate contour of very narrow scope. The rhythmic pattern is sufficiently metrical to be called versified, whilst the dynamic variation is minimal and invention entirely lacking. Whatever may be said about the Symphony as a whole hardly anything can be said about its theme.

Why?

There are two interdependent reasons, one musical and the other poetic. The musical reason becomes clear as the work unfolds, for in it the theme undergoes no real process of development. Many subsequent themes are inspired by it, but the true development takes place in the background. The *idée* itself, therefore, must possess sufficient anonymity to suffer repetition without strain. It must be present but never violently active. For such a role the *Harold* theme is perfectly cast.

The poetic reason is similar. The only possible connection between the course of this symphony and the events of Byron's *Childe Harold* lies in the similar characters and behaviour of Berlioz' tune and Byron's hero. Both are chameleon-like, drifting and for-ever becoming part of the changing scene about them. Here is a perfect fusion of poetic *idée* with musical structure, the mysterious source of that *genre instrumental expressif* for which Berlioz always sought, and which he so often discovered.

LA DAMNATION DE FAUST: ROMANCE

Now, compare this almost equally conventional-type melody with the *Harold* theme just discussed. At first sight it might appear to come from any French opera of the period. On closer inspection however, it reveals itself to be characteristically Berliozian.

Ten bars fall into five equal phrases beneath a late-climax lemniscate curve of no great scope. The rhythmic pattern is hardly subtle and no dynamic variation is indicated, at least not in the vocal line. But there are several important points of difference between these two themes. Each of the five phrases in the *Romance* starts with an upbeat: it does get away from the tonic key for a short time by passing into the supertonic in phrase three: and its upward leap of a ninth in the second phrase gives it a force of character purposely absent from the *Harold* theme. Overriding all these perhaps, is its general relationship to the tonic note. The *Harold* theme hovered around its tonic, but Marguerite's line moves outwards from it. Such a melody has a sense of great freedom, and since the interval between its first and its climactic notes is a little wider than that of the *Harold* theme, its root character will be that much more assertive, forceful and definite.

Although the over-all climax-point is late (bar seven), the climax of each phrase is immediate, occurring always upon the second note. Thus the shape of each constituent phrase is directly opposed to that of the whole tune. This sets up a linear tension which is constant throughout the ten bars, and which enhances its basic strength and concentration. Marguerite is not vague: nor does she vacillate in the manner of the *fantastique*'s hero. She is positively and desperately unhappy.

Her state of mind is underlined by the characteristic emphasis on one rhythmic figure in the accompaniment ♪♪ ₇ ♪♪ ₇ ♪♪ ₇ Figures such as this were often associated with intensely tragic or sorrowful situations in Berlioz' music, and it matters little whether we regard them as heart-beats or as semiquavers. The important point is that Berlioz knew rhythm to be one of music's most expressive elements, largely neglected as such by contemporary composers, and he exploited this knowledge to the full. Another significant fact is the location of all such illustrative figures in the accompanying orchestral parts. The possibilities for dramatic and expressive illustration, and for emotional concentration, afforded by the accompaniment in opera, cantata and song had been one of the great discoveries of the Baroque age, striking a sympathetic chord in the minds of most French composers from the time of Rameau onwards. In the expressive rhythmic subtleties of Berlioz' operatic and instrumental music the Gallic concern for metre, scansion and rhetorical modulation received its Romantic apotheosis. Permanent principles of musical expressiveness were set free from ephemeral formal schemes and inspired a whole new world of expressive sound.

Reference has already been made to another of Berlioz' melodic habits in which the several limbs of a simple tune take unexpected tonal directions after beginning in a similar or conventional way. The best known of such tunes is perhaps the *Marche des Pèlerins* from *Harold en Italie*, a movement of which we shall have occasion to speak at a later stage and in a slightly different context. But an equally interesting case is afforded by our next example, the *Prière* from *Benvenuto Cellini*.

BENVENUTO CELLINI: PRIÈRE

This fascinating melody is typical of the deliberate coolness of so much of Berlioz' most deeply-felt music. Twenty-three bars long, its five phrases are exquisitely balanced, possessing a truly classical poise which expects its god to meet it half-way. There is neither subservience nor defiance here: just a deeply-felt plea expressed in quietly reasonable terms. Its setting in a rumbustious opera has nothing to do with its own inherent quality and design, although it reflects vividly upon the structural potential of the perennial French doctrine of contrast, opposition and effect. The bar ratio-pattern—4:4:4:4:7—perfectly illustrates this balanced reasonableness, as does the pattern of rise, fall and hover created by the contours of the three lines of which it consists. Particularly noteworthy is the last seven-bar phrase, which floats appealingly as though expecting some reply.

The strange pattern of modulation which informs this *Prière* is the direct result of Berlioz' tonal thinking, and it is fascinating to see how effective it can be on so small a scale. The first line ends in *D*, the key of the flattened seventh. The second line takes us to *G*, the key on the minor third: whilst the final line, with due emphasis upon the chord of the minor subdominant, returns us quite comfortably to the home key of *E*.

The second verse continues the tonally exploratory character of the first, its opening lines moving to *C* and *F*, the keys of the flattened submediant and the flattened supertonic respectively.

Fusion of the alternative modes on the tonic *E*—Berlioz' most significant contribution to the tonal language, and one which we shall deal with fully in another chapter—allows him to assemble all these keys beneath one extended melodic arc without discomfort or strain, opening up new vistas in the tonal system and fresh dimensions in the art of expressive melodic composition.

The texture of the accompaniment is simple, contrasting straightforward harmonization of a tune with a repeated rhythmic pattern. Its fundamental conception and structure—activity contrasted with rest—is similar to that of the *fantastique* theme, whilst the background procession of pilgrims emphasizes the similarity of both feeling and method which exists between this *Prière* and the *Marche des Pèlerins* from *Harold en Italie*.

The deliberate manner in which Berlioz composed his music, planning the smallest details of its structure and shape in accordance with his varying expressive intentions should by now be making itself increasingly clear. But nowhere is it more obvious than in the next two examples, taken from *Le Corsaire* and the *Prélude* to *Les Troyens à Carthage*.

LE CORSAIRE

The main tune from this Overture is as simple and direct a melody as Berlioz ever wrote. Of sixteen bars duration (tempo direction *Allegro assai*), and lacking any complexity of phrasing whatsoever (bar ratio-pattern 4:4:4:4), its expressive intentions—rumbustiousness with a touch of the vulgar—are as obvious as is its symmetrical outline. The contrast of arpeggio with scale, and of descent with ascent, makes it an almost pure example *en clair* of some of the basic terms in Berlioz' melodic vocabulary, whilst the manner in which the contour of the first eight bars is inverted in that of bars nine to sixteen, reveals that deliberateness of fashioning which is fast becoming the most noticeable feature of Berlioz' compositional method. Its convenience for canonic treatment is obvious, underlining Berlioz' little-publicized instinct for counterpoint. Although he never wrote a fugue as such after his student days, his music is filled with contrapuntal passages of great skill, dexterity and expressive power.

The texture which accompanies the initial presentation of the theme is quite commonplace. Generally the harmonies are sustained by the wood-winds, whilst the rhythmic drive is provided by conventional sextuplet quaverings in the upper strings, and dramatic colour infused by the brass family. Like the *ideé fixe* in *Harold en Italie* its straightforward character allows it to be heard against differing background textures from the *oom-pah-pah-pah* variety upwards.

The fact that it is played on the bass instruments is also significant. The gradual emancipation of the bass line had been in its day one of the signs of the growing maturity of the Classical language in music, and a sign of the confidence with which composers were able to speak it. Living when he did Berlioz inherited both this maturity and this sense of confidence: and being French—a people whose musical speech and artistic ideals retained many old and hallowed principles—his melodies were not confined to the upper parts of his textures. In Berlioz' music themes migrate and may appear in any part or parts. This had considerable effects on his harmonic grammar, as we shall discover at a later stage, and partly accounts for the individual sonority of his scores.

LES TROYENS A CARTHAGE: PRÉLUDE

This curious orchestral *Prélude*—French musical Republicanism at its most refined—has an austerity of sound matched only by the severity of its formal construction. Nothing else in Berlioz is quite like it, and it is certainly superior to anything in this *genre* written by any other composer of the time.

Thirty-six bars long, its phrases move in a thrice stated bar ratio-pattern of 3:3:6. Every phrase starts on a downbeat and all are of very narrow range. No phrase save the last exceeds a major sixth in scope, and the span of this is but an octave. In fact the whole thirty-six bar melody is contained within the compass of a ninth. It must surely be one of the narrowest extended melodies ever written.

The pattern of intervallic expansion and contraction, and the interwoven apposition of leap and line, is fascinating. After hovering about a tone for almost two bars, the first phrase leaps a major sixth. This is balanced by the second phrase which descends through a fourth by step. The third phrase hovers about a semitone for almost four bars, and then leaps a minor sixth. In its turn this is balanced by a stepwise fall through a minor third: but this time the hover, leap and fall are all contained within one continuous line. The fourth phrase leaps a perfect fifth after fluctuating about a semitone, whilst its answering phrase falls from B♭ to G♯ via the intermediate note *A*. Phrase six, with an over-all scope of a diminished fifth, opens and closes with steps, confining its wider intervallic motion to the inner bards. Phrases seven and eight are identical with phrases one and two, whilst the final phrase begins by stepping upwards from middle *D* to the octave above. It closes with a falling minor sixth and rising perfect fourth, relieved in the first instance by a downward semitone step, and in the second by the last three notes of the *F* major scale in typical Republican rhythm.

The contours of the phrases form a geometrical pattern which can only be described as cool, so low is the tension of the conflict amongst themselves, and between them and the theme's over-all late-climax lemniscate curve. The full geometrical construction of this melody is best illustrated graphically.

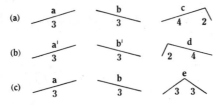

In Berlioz' music there is no valid distinction to be drawn between intelligence and feeling, form and material. Musical syntax and affective metaphor are fused into one expressive whole appropriate to the current emotional situation. What could be more suited to a Classical tragedy than a *Prélude* created along such lines as these? With its disciplined but basically assertive general outline and its acutely balanced and contrasted shapes of phrase, it is surely one of the most expressive musical lines ever penned.

The curious austerity of its sound is enhanced by the highly individual orchestral texture in which the line is set. It was not technical incompetence which led Berlioz to make such a strange outlay of his instrumental forces, but an acute appreciation of the quality of ancient life as he felt it portrayed in Classical writings. It is a perfect translation into French musical terms of the texture of the heroic events which follow it, and it leaves all other contemporary historical posturings far behind. Although it owes much to Gluck in the musical field, its real inspiration springs from a powerful and sympathetic creative imagination which felt itself at one with the circumstances of the dramatic action. As he himself said on more than one occasion during his lifetime, Berlioz really understood and suffered with these people: and his understanding shines through the music in which he portrayed them.

No discussion of Berlioz' melodic lines would be complete without reference to a particular type of linear pattern characteristic of much French music, and of music influenced by French taste, from early times to the present day. Frequently encountered in Berlioz' works, it is a line of ever-increasing or ever-decreasing leaps, either away from or towards a particular repeated note. It is a Baroque-style line, a perennial tool of the operatic *genre*, and its expressive quality and force is great—assertive, growing in musical tension and dramatic intensity in the former arrangement: subsiding, relaxing the tension and the intensity in the latter.

Immensely adaptable, capable of great extension or contraction, easily recognizable and therefore of great formal value, it is the fruit of both intelligence and feeling: and Berlioz uses this pattern for large-scale structural ends as well as for more limited melodic cohesion and musically expressive purposes. The subtle interpenetration of leap and line, so characteristic of his melodic writing as a whole, is here raised to its ultimate point. In a way it is the most Berliozian of all possible musical lines. A few examples of its appearance in his works are given here in both its pure and decorated forms, in both its melodic and more extended structural functions.

MELODIC BUILDING

The evidence assembled in the foregoing pages seems to show that Berlioz built up his melodies by a systematic manipulation of basic, expressive phrase-shapes, a technique as old as melody itself, and one which amounts almost to a personal *doctrine of affections*. The fact that this *can* be said, regardless of whether he himself was fully aware of it or not, only goes to demonstrate the reality of that sympathy with Baroque principles and conceptions which appears to inform French music and critical writings generally, as well as his own works in particular. In this sense he was one of the most comprehensive musicians ever to set pen to manuscript paper, with more genuine historical sympathy and understanding within his nature than any of his contemporaries. As a result his melodies possess a malleable plasticity which is at heart anonymous. What ciphers may have been to Schumann, the sense of plastic shapeliness undoubtedly was to Berlioz: and once more one calls to mind the statement of A. W. von Schlegel that this sense of the plastic was the essential ingredient of Ancient art, the main point of difference between it and the art of the modern world. Of how much of this he was fully conscious remains a moot point. But that he had some inkling of his own creative methods is revealed by a paragraph in a letter he once wrote to Bennet, a paragraph which is quoted by that most sympathetic of French writers, Romain Rolland, in his book *Musicians of Today*, and which is given now.

You make me laugh with your old words about a mission to fulfil. What a missionary! But there is within me an inexplicable mechanism [*sic*] which works in spite of all arguments; and I let it work because I cannot stop it.

It is of course true that in this passage Berlioz was speaking more generally than the sense in which I am inclined to read it. But it can bear a more detailed and precise application: and his use of the word *mechanism* carries a greater significance than most full-blooded Romantics might care to admit. But then Berlioz was so much more than a full-blooded Romantic, and his life-long solitariness was as much due to this fact as ever it was to the idiosyncrasies of his own character.

In this connection I cannot refrain from mentioning a story told by Auguste Barbier in his *Souvenirs personnels et Silhouettes contemporaines*. Berlioz and he had together attended the funeral of a mutual friend. During the ceremony, and at the very graveside itself, Berlioz had shown no emotion whatsoever. But the obsequies being concluded, the poet and the musician returned to Berlioz' house for tea and a reading of Shakespeare's *Hamlet*. As, striding about his room, the composer declaimed the play, uncontrollable tears began to flow until he was in the last extremity of emotional *frisson*. As Barbier remarked, that which the tragedies of life could never draw from Berlioz' heart was set free by the monuments of Art. We should do well to remember this when we consider his music.

Leaving aside the special case of what I have called a typically Gallic melodic line, let us recall the examples which have been used in this chapter. Every one of them exhibits an arrangement of phrases constructed from rising and falling lines which group themselves into four basic and recurring types. Although the variation in detail is almost infinite, these four basic shapes may be illustrated graphically as follows:

(a)   (b)   (c)   (d)

and described verbally as symmetrical: late-climax lemniscate: early-climax lemniscate: and hovering. All are subject to inversion. What is true of the individual phrase-shapes is true also of the melodic contours as wholes, with one notable exception. None of Berlioz' melodies possesses an over-all contour which hovers. All of them therefore may be classified under one or other of the first three general headings.

The significant fact in all this is the apparently firm alliance between a particular contour and a particular, though generalized, expressive intention. All symmetrical contours convey an emotion which, like *Le Corsaire,* is neither deeply introspective nor yet reaching for the stars. Those whose curve is a late-climax lemniscate are assertive and outgoing, the general intensity of their feeling being dependent upon the height and speed of their climb. Thus the intensity of the *idée fixe* in the *Symphonie fantastique* is much greater than that of its counterpart in *Harold en Italie*. On the other hand, introspection of varying degrees is expressed through melodic lines which trace an early-climax lemniscate curve, lines such as that which opens *Roméo seul,* or which make up the love theme in the same work.

The complexity of human emotion is conveyed by the extent to which the individual phrase-shapes within any melodic line either agree with, or run counter to, one another and to the over-all contour of the whole. Thus, taken together, the variety of phrase-shapes within the over-all late-climax lemniscate curve of the *fantastique* theme create a perfect and comprehensive musical symbol for the irresolute character of the supposed hero/heroine: whilst the extreme tension within Marguerite's breast is given full musical expression through the opposition of all the individual phrase-shapings to that of the whole melodic line. Nor is this all. Further modifications of expressive intensity will be produced by the number of the phrases, the regularity or otherwise of their bar ratio-pattern, and the over-all length or shortness of the whole. Some indication of the relationship between all these factors and the nature of their resultant expressive colouring can be given by listing the characteristics of certain melodies, as in the following table.

Work	Bars	Phrases	Ratio-pattern
Symphonie fantastique	40	8	8:7:4:4:4:5:2:6
Roméo Seul	21	7	2:2:4:2:2:4:4
Symphonie funèbre (*a*)	19	5	2:2:2:4:9
(*b*)	30	11	4:2:2:5:1:4:3:2:2:2:3
Harold en Italie	8	2	4:4
Romance (Faust)	10	5	2:2:2:2:2
Prière (Cellini)	23	5	4:4:4:4:7
Le Corsaire	16	4	4:4:4:4
Prélude (Les Troyens)	36	9	3:3:6 ⎫ 3:3:6 ⎬ 3:3:6 ⎭

The advantage of such a method of analysis—I do not say system, since of all composers Berlioz was the most antipathetic to such things—is its open-endedness. The composer's invention and the listener's tenacity to one side, there is no reason why melodies created in this way should not go on for ever. Nor does there seem to be any end to the number of contrasts which they may contain. Even when they have less exalted goals than infinity or total emotional comprehensiveness, they are unlikely to conform to the established rhyming schemes of more conventional and metrical tunes. Thus Berlioz' melodies are extended and asymmetrical because these characteristics are part of their very nature. The expressive character of his art demands it so. He is not out to astonish the bourgeoisie, but to express, in wholly musical terms, the plenitude of contrasts which taken together make up Life as the Romantics felt it. In many ways this had also been Shakespeare's aim, and it is not surprising that the Romantic sensibility believed a natural sympathy to exist between itself and the poet of the first Elizabethan age. Nor, conversely, is it surprising that the kind of mind which could dismiss *Othello* as a 'bloody farce' because it ignored the supposed Unities of Aristotle, or which would rewrite *Hamlet* because the gravedigger behaved in a somewhat unseemly fashion, could also, in its nineteenth- and early twentieth-century reincarnations, question both the existence of Berlioz' melodic lines and the validity of his artistic competence.

⌈3⌉

Berlioz and Tonality

T HE DETAILS OF BERLIOZ' TONAL PROCEDURES SHOW
but a quantitative advance upon those of Beethoven.
Everything which Berlioz did had been anticipated or
hinted at by the earlier composer, though less frequently and with
less persistence. Berlioz built upon the past as he saw it through his
own very Gallic eyes. Consequently the fundamental relationship
of tonic to dominant and of tonic to relative, underlay all his
sonata-type structures, as the following selected list will show.

Symphonie fantastique	C — G — C
Symphonie funèbre	f — A♭ — f
Les Francs-Juges	f — A♭ — f
Waverley	D — A — D
Le Roi Lear	C — G — C
Carnaval romain	A — E — A
Le Corsaire	C — G — C
Benvenuto Cellini (Overture)	G — D — G

But he did widen the tonal field lying between these focal points,
lingering over those relationships which Beethoven and his contemporaries had treated transiently, and giving each an expressive
musical importance of its own. Although this greatly increased the
colour and excitement of his music, the resultant complexity under-
mined the process of extended modulation which was the main
pivot of the old and simpler system. Thus, although the basic
relationships were kept, their prime function was obscured, and
from this a certain weakness of structure almost invariably resulted.
His most successful 'sonata' movements, therefore, were those
which, from the tonal point of view, were his least characteristic—
the first movements of the *Symphonie fantastique* and the *Symphonie
funèbre*, for instance—whilst his most individually-conceived
'sonata' schemes—movements such as the second part of the *Orgie*

from *Harold en Italie*—were inclined to collapse beneath the weight
of the number of tonalities they encompassed. Berlioz is at his best
when his formal schemes are as personal as his language, when
the characteristic shifts of semitone, tone, minor third or major
third, themselves create the structures through which they work.
The *Dignare Domine* section of the *Te Deum* is a first-class example
of new musical wine in a new formal bottle; whilst movements
such as the *Angels' Chorus* in *L'Enfance du Christ* show how the
initially dialectical hypothesis of tonic to dominant can be turned
to a truly poetic purpose provided that the 'sonata' scheme is
eschewed. One of the more interesting aspects of the Romantic
period in general, and of French Romanticism in particular, is its
inherent sympathy with older, pre-Classical techniques and turns
of musical phrase, expressed in tonal, harmonic and structural
terms as well as in those of scholarship and general emotional
attitudes. The adaptation of *ritornello* structure which informs *La
Course à l'Abîme* in *Faust*, for instance, shows how pre-sonata
formal principles possessed sufficient flexibility to sustain the post-
sonata language. On reflection this should not surprise us, since the
ultimate ground of the sympathy which the Romantics felt for
their Baroque and earlier predecessors lay in the common richness
of their several musical languages. This last is the crux of the
Romanticist's problem and the source of his constant formal
difficulties.

Although Berlioz never codified the basic premises of his own
language, examination and analysis of his works reveals that these
can be summed up in the form of a semi-chromatic and ambimodal
scale which makes full use of all the elements of both major and
minor modes, including the flattened seventh, in any one tonality.
Thus, in the key of G for instance, tonal shifts could be made
between any of the following eleven key areas, and each of these
could itself be in either the major or the minor mode.

Both the strength and the weakness of this system lies in the
retention, unalloyed, of the old focal points of dominant and
sub-dominant. On the credit side this combined stability with
change, opening up exciting new paths without destroying the
old. But on the debit side it created a tension between linguistic

richness and grammatical clarity which could not help but pro-
mote the eventual dissolution of the tonal system. It was for this
reason that Berlioz' main contribution to the art of music was in
the realm of syntax. He added greatly to its grammatical possibilities without increasing its harmonic vocabulary by a single new
chord as such. An achievement of this order is necessarily solitary and demanding, for it requires a creative approach to formal
problems which not every Romantic composer was able to fulfil.
Thus, the chief interest of his works from the present point of
view lies more in his methods than in their sonorous results, and
it is an examination of these in the tonal and harmonic fields which
will be the main concern of this and the following chapter.

Stimulated no doubt by the examples of Reicha and Beethoven, Berlioz made tonal relationships of a third his most common procedure. In this his path was eased by the well known and
constantly used movement between tonic and relative, as well as
that more recently exploited shift between tonic and flattened submediant. It is interesting to note that in his *Histoire du Romantisme*
(Paris 1829) F. R. de Toreinx considered Beethoven's increasing
use of the key on the flattened sixth to be evidence of Romantic
feeling in music. To these Berlioz added the relationship of major
tonic to flattened mediant, and all the introductory sections of the
Overtures listed above probe one or other of these shifts.

Les Francs-juges	f–D♭	i–♭VI
Waverley	D–F–D	I–♭III–I
Le Roi Lear	Cc–E♭–cC	Ii–♭III–iI
Carnaval romain	A–C–A	I–♭III–I
Le Corsaire	c–A♭	i–♭VI
Benvenuto Cellini	G–E♭–G	I–♭VI–I

Such relationships need not remain simple, and one of the great
advantages of music fashioned from the comprehensive scale
outlined above, especially in matters of expressive colouring, is its
ability to move easily both to and from keys on both its major and
its minor thirds. The structural potential of this is great, and is to
be seen in the large-scale tonal planning of many of Berlioz'
movements and works. The Overture *Carnaval romain*, for instance, appears to be in the key of *A major*: but its first modulation in the introductory section is to *C*, the key on the *minor* third
of the tonic scale. This inclusive modality is reflected in the body

of the movement, where a passage presented initially as a contrasting of the chords of *A* and *C majors*,

appears later on as a contrast between the chords of *A major* and
c sharp minor.

Thus, the chords on both possible thirds in the fundamental
tonality of *A* have been employed, structurally as well as expressively.

In the *Easter Hymn* from *La Damnation de Faust,* a movement in
the over-all tonality of *F* major can move easily and logically to
A♭, the major key on the tonic's *minor* third. And this can be
offset, harmonically, by the appearance of the chord of *A* major in
the cadential passage.

(a)

(b)

One of the clearest examples of the structural influence wielded by modal inclusiveness is seen in the *Quaerens me* section of the *Grande Messe des Morts*. The whole movement is built on the alternative thirds (*C* and *C♯*) of the tonality of *A*. Going first to the dominant key, *E* major, it cadences in the key of *C*. This is at once followed by a passage ending in *c♯* minor. Thus, in the space of forty-nine bars, the triads of both major and minor modes of *A* have been involved in extended tonal outline.

$$A \text{ - } E \text{ - } C \text{ - } c\sharp$$

Even more interesting is the vocal *Scherzetto* from *Roméo et Juliette*, where the structure of the whole movement depends upon tonal shifts between its tonic area, *F*, and the keys on its alternative thirds (*A♭* and *A*) and sixths (*D♭* and *D*). The plan appears thus.

```
F  - a  - d  - A♭      I  - iii - vi - ♭III
F♭ - D♭ - F  - a  - F  I i - ♭VI - I  - iii - I
```

The mastery of the principles of tonal structure which designs such as these display should offset the common view which, acknowledging Berlioz' gifts as an expressive musical colourist yet denies him any true understanding or control of poetically inspired form. In tonal music, however wide its field of action, colourful orchestration cannot reinforce weak structure, though it may largely compensate for it. If Berlioz had been no more than a supremely gifted orchestrator, it is doubtful whether his works would have borne so well the brunt of more than a century's misunderstanding.

The characteristic and extended chains of tertial relationships, moving beyond the limits of the alternative thirds and sixths, arise quite naturally from Berlioz' approach to formal problems, and they may sustain sections of a piece, whole movements, or even make up the focal points in the framework of the greater part of an entire composition. The first of these procedures, working on a relatively large scale has already been noted in the A–C–E– plan of the introductory section of *Carnaval romain*. But its appearance on a wider front is seen in the framework created by the main key areas of the majority of the movements in both the *Symphonie fantastique* and *Harold en Italie*.

Symphonic fantastique cC–A–F–g–C (3 out of 5 movements)
Harold en Italie   gG–E–C–gG (3 out of 4 movements)

On a smaller and more self-contained scale the first twenty-eight bars of *La Damnation de Faust* create a similar plan. The whole is within the general *ambiance* of D major, a mode confirmed by the inner tonal changes which progress from D to f♯ minor, to A major, to c♯ minor and back to D once more. It is worth noting, however, the slight infusion of the minor mode in bar six through the medium of the flattened sixth note, and the similar and balancing colouring of the dominant phrases by the appearance of an F natural.

Another instance of extended tertial movement, this time in a fugato texture—Reicha's favourite method in Reicha's favoured texture, but now successfully employed—is to be heard at the very opening of *Roméo et Juliette*. Here, every voice after the second enters in the key a third higher than that of its predecessor.

(*b*)–G–b–D–f♯

But perhaps the purest and most consistent example of tertial procedure in all his works is that furnished by the *Dignare Domine* section of the *Te Deum*. The whole structure is made up of balanced movement in thirds, at first ascending from *D* major to *E♭* major, and then descending from *E* major to its home point of *D*.

Dd–F–a–Cc–E♭e♭   Ii–♭III–v–♭VII–♭II

E–c♯–A–f♯–D   II–vii–V–iii–I

This movement is an almost perfect demonstration of the reality of the ambimodal ground which I have suggested informs and sustains Berlioz' musical language, for it involves both modes upon the tonic and the dominant, as well as both modes upon the flattened supertonic and the minor seventh: and it treats the alternative supertonics, thirds and sevenths as roots in their own right.

Most examples of tertial tonal relationships, however, short-term or long-range, exhibit a discrete structure in which two or more sets of thirds, not themselves a third apart, are arranged in juxtaposition. Of such an arrangement, on a vast scale and informing a whole work, the tonal plan of the main sections in *Roméo et Juliette* provides a fine example.

b–G: F–F–A–F: eE–C♯ : E♭(D♯)–D–B

On a much smaller scale the internal arrangement of the *Prologue* for Chorus and orchestra from the same work is similarly conceived.

Chorus: *Orchestra:*   *Chorus:*

b–dD–f♯–A ‖   A–F   ‖   F–D: a–C–Ee (Next movement—G).

This is a clear example of the way in which Berlioz' ambimodal language makes à basically conventional shift from *b* to *Ee* peculiarly personal. To begin with the extremities are both given minor colouring. Then, what could have been accomplished almost immediately in the space of a few measures is extended by tertial progression until it occupies no less than ninety-eight bars, includes four changes of time-signature as well as numerous alterations of tempo and style, and involves at least ten real changes of key or mode. True, the secure establishing of a new key area even in the most conventional language nearly always requires an approach from its own dominant. But Berlioz' tactics are those of a musical siege. Some would call it inflation and be well aware of the pejorative overtones of the word. But they would be wrong: for the music both *qua* music and *qua* expressiveness requires every one of these elements. Only in this way could the classical language, fashioned largely for the purposes of tonal dialectic, become sufficiently responsive to the demands of Romantic poeticism that it could continue to develop. Only in this way could it become an appropriate tool for contemporary musical sensibility. Looked at from this point of view, the tonal plan and formal extension of the *Prologue* to *Roméo et Juliette* is an example not of riotous inflation but of that most French of all artistic qualities, masterful economy.

Other movements, though of a basically tertial nature, display a more complex plan. An excellent example of this is the *Oraison funèbre* from the *Symphonie funèbre et triomphale*, in which a broad shift from *e* minor to *G* major is surrounded with tonal *chiaroscuro* involving at least six other keys. The movement's prime structural and expressive function is to link, through contrast, those on either side of it which, like those at the extremities of the *Prologue* discussed above, are a fifth apart.

It begins with the chord of *B♭*—the subdominant of the previous tonality—which, by changing first its mode and then the spelling of its fundamental note, carries the music into *e* minor through a series of alternating diminished and dominant seventh chords erected upon the notes *B♭*, *A♯*, *A♮*, and *B*.

The *e* minor tonality is then confirmed by a further series of diminished and dominant sevenths, after which the instrumental *récitatif* on the solo trombone moves from that key to *a* minor, *C* major and *G* major, coming to rest at last upon the chord of *c* minor. A diminished seventh in that key gives way to a dominant seventh on the note *B*, and the passage cadences in *E* major. In this last key the next section, *Andantino*, begins. After passing into *d* minor the mode changes to the major, which acts as a dominant chord introducing the *Oraison* proper in *G*.

In this more precise section the tonal and harmonic plan is finely balanced. It begins by moving upwards in thirds, from *G* major through *b* minor to *D* major, and follows this with a further move in the same direction through a sequence of two fifths, from *D* major to *e* minor. Tertial movement is then resumed in the passage from *e* minor to *B♭* major via *G* major, in which key ultimately it rests.

If we now draw an abstract of the tonal changes described above we shall be able to see at a glance how Berlioz combined the old methods with the new. Tertial movement is relieved by movement in fifths and preceded by that dependent upon a descending chromatic line. Known facts are put into a new framework of reference, and an entirely fresh sound results.

After movement in thirds, tonal change by step or by a series of steps is Berlioz' most favoured procedure. An example of the simplest possible of all such stepping movement is heard in the opening pages of *L'Enfance du Christ*. Here, a single held note in the voice part changes its tonal significance during its course from tonic to leading-note. Thus the music passes comfortably from *E♭* to *E* major.

Somewhat more brusque in effect is our next example—from the Overture *Le Corsaire*. In this passage chromatic alteration of the note *C* to *C*♯, combined with one of Berlioz' favourite and most individually used chords, the diminished seventh, is sufficient to twist the tonality into *D*♭ major, the key of the flattened supertonic.

Berlioz often used this key of the flattened supertonic as a transient tonal centre, and a small-scale example of this Neapolitan modulation is to be heard in the following extract from a recitative in *La Damnation de Faust*. Here, in the key of *B*♭ major, the subdominant chord gives way to that of the flattened supertonic by means of an enharmonic change wrung upon the note *E*♭, turning it into *D*♯. Later, the chord of *B* major is re-spelt as the chord of *C*♭, and treated in a thoroughly conventional manner, so that the whole line cadences easily in the tonic key.

Another example of tonal movement by a semitone, only this time in a downward direction and of a greater extension, is provided by the song *Le Spectre de la Rose* from *Nuits d'Été*. In this example, a piece which begins in B major arrives in B♭ major after twenty-one bars, remaining in the new tonal area for ten bars before returning to the original tonic.

Our final example is taken from the famous but somewhat hollow *Orgie* which forms the last movement of *Harold en Italie*. Here, the *Allegro* following the *Souvenir de l'Introduction* moves from g minor to f♯ minor, settling in F♯ major for the *Souvenir de la Marche des Pèlerins*. After this, a further change of mode carries the

music back to *G* major for the *Souvenir de la Sérénade*. The whole
passage extends across eighteen bars.

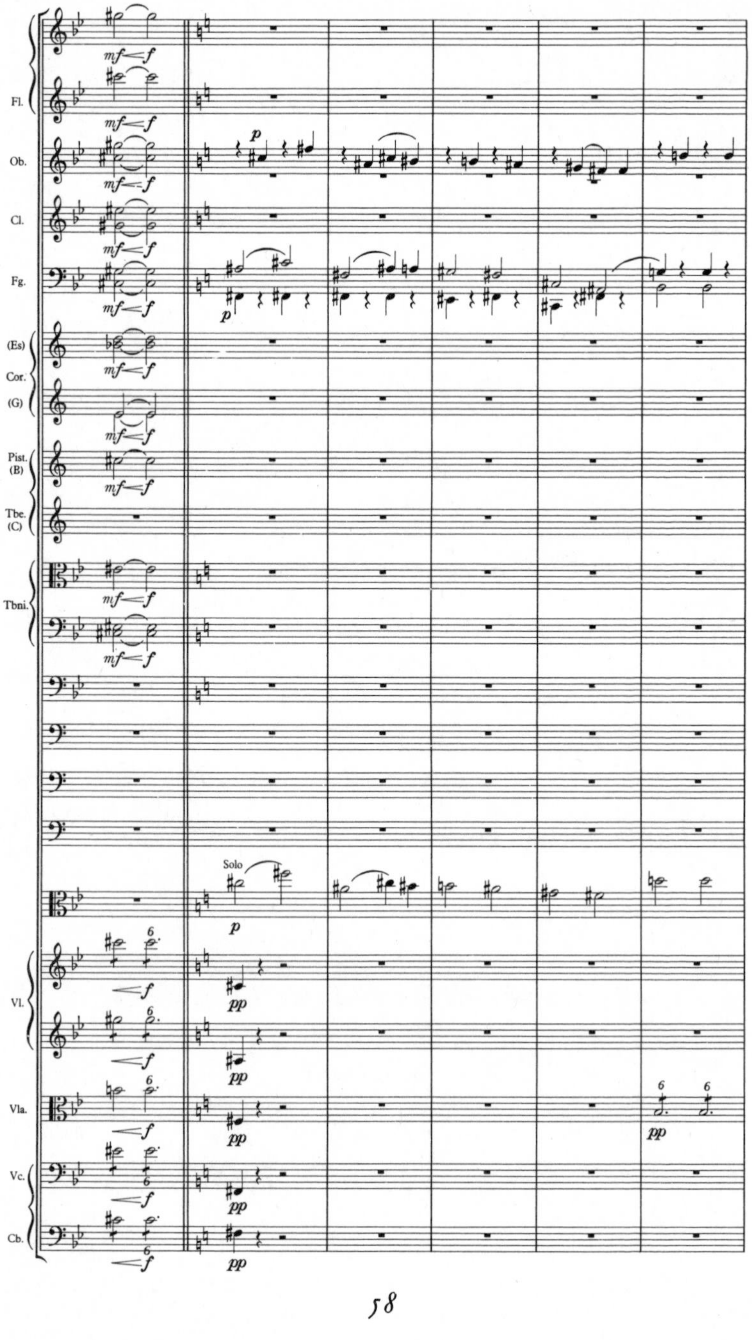
Fl.
Ob.
Cl.
Fg.
(Es)
Cor.
(G)
Pist.
(B)
Tbe.
(C)
Tbni.
Solo
Vl.
Vla.
Vc.
Cb.
mf
f
p
pp

59

(Souvenir de la Serenade.)

An example in miniature of complex movement by steps—representative of the many such shifts to be found in a host of Berlioz' structures, and on a variety of different scales—is provided by the following short passage from the beginning of Part Two in *La Damnation de Faust*. Here, movement downwards by a tone (D to C) is followed immediately by that of a semitone in the opposite direction (C to c♯ minor). The immediate inspiration in this case is obviously poetic for it arises from the text to which it is set, *Qui vient d'étendre au loin son silence et ses voiles*. But the grammatical construction possesses its own validity.

The manner in which two discrete sets of thirds can be locked together by the kind of single semitone step which we have been discussing is nowhere more clearly seen than in the *Dignare Domine* section of the *Te Deum*, already referred to on page 52.

At the point where the ascending chain of thirds meets its descending counterpart there is a change of tonality from E♭ to E, identical in its basic method with that described on pages 54–5, in the example from *L'Enfance du Christ*. Once more the note E♭

changes its tonal significance from tonic to leading-note and, be-coming *D♯*, guides the music smoothly into *E*. The method is as moving as the music, and the intelligence of the whole conception is equalled only by the nobility of its sound.

More extended tonal movement by a series of upward or downward steps is also a common feature of Berlioz' compositional technique, and its presence in the *idée fixe* of the *Symphonie fantastique* has already been mentioned in the previous chapter. A similar example, also contained within the theme itself and therefore also on a relatively small scale, is found in the Overture *Le Roi Lear*.

This is a Romantic application of a tonal procedure common to much music of the diatonic period. In earlier times it tended to be restricted to passages that were basically modulatory or episodic. But since the later part of the eighteenth century its appearance as an integral part of thematic material, especially in operatic aria and dramatic recitative, had been frequent. A very large number of High-Classical and early-Romantic instrumental themes exploit it also, two of the best-known examples being the main themes in the opening movements of Beethoven's First Symphony and Schubert's Eighth. But in both of these instances the movement is of one step only, from tonic to supertonic and eventually back again. As with so many other known and tried procedures, Berlioz expanded it for his own expressive, musical purposes, and the following group of examples will show how frequently, with what degrees of subtlety and for what differing expressive reasons he made use of it.

Rising tonal steps increase the tension of the music, which tension can be humorous or eager as well as tragic, as the following extracts from Act Two of *Benvenuto Cellini*, and from the first song in *Nuits d'Été* show. In the former the inn-keeper holds the centre of the stage: and as he recites the lengthy list of wines already drunk by Cellini's companions but not yet paid for, his music moves from *g* minor, through *a* minor to *b♭* minor.

In the following example the rising excitement of springtime is reflected in the tonal contour of the first part of the *Villanelle*, which ascends by steps from *A* to *F* majors.

A–B♭–b–c♯–(D)–e–F

sous   nos   pieds é gre nant les   par les

Another example (also to do with drinking, but this time of a solitary and more ominous kind) precedes the *Easter Hymn* in *La Damnation de Faust*, in which Faust's music moves upwards from *b* minor to *d* minor, via *C* and *D♭* majors.

A truly remarkable example of this stepping procedure, extended, organic and extremely effective, opens the so-called development section of the first movement in the *Symphonie fantastique*. Within the space of twenty-six bars a thoroughly conventional modulation from the dominant to the tonic keys is carried by two sets of steps, both starting in *G*. The first set leads to *B♭* through *A♭* major and *a* minor, whilst the second set arrives in *C* major by omitting the move to *A♭* and going straight through *a* minor and *B♭* major.

Extended tonal movement in downward steps is, perhaps, not quite so common as its opposite: but it is equally effective, and produces a highly individual sound. This is shown by the following three examples, taken from the first movement of the *Symphonie funèbre et triomphale*, the *Christe Rex Gloriae* section of the *Te Deum*, and from *Brander's song* in *La Damnation de Faust*.

In the first, a softly played cadence in $A\flat$ major concluding one section is immediately followed by a *fortissimo* chord of E major and a unison passage in that key ending on the dominant note. This is succeeded by an equally loud chord of $e\flat$ minor, and a shorter line in the same key. In its turn this gives way to a *fortissimo* chord of $D\flat$ major which, after being confirmed by an arpeggio, falls onto the chord of C major, the dominant of the fundamental key (f minor), to which the music shortly returns. From a long-term point of view the whole passage is a conventional shift from the mediant to the relative minor tonic. But it is achieved in a thoroughly Berliozian fashion, through descending steps.

$A\flat–E–e\flat–D\flat–(C)–f$

In the second example, diminished seventh leads to diminished seventh in the key of *e* minor, *d* minor and *c* minor.

Finally, in Brander's song, the beginning of each line in every verse is pitched one step down from that of its predecessor, the initial shift being of a tone and the others of a semitone each.

> D–A
> C–G
> b–F
> B♭–D

An amplification of movement by step, and one of Berlioz' most original tonal structures, is the *Marche des Pèlerins* from *Harold en Italie*. Whatever this movement may have owed in general inspiration to the ever-popular *Allegretto* from Beethoven's Seventh Symphony, its tonal organization is quite different from anything that Beethoven had conceived. In the contour described by its focal points it is essentially Gallic, describing that somewhat athletic and wiry line of ever-increasing leaps which, in one of its many possible melodic forms, is common to so many of Berlioz' works.

The *Marche* consists of three significantly altered presentations of the theme, interleaved with a reminiscence of the *idée fixe* on the solo viola, and a *canto religioso* on the muted strings. The number of limbs in each presentation is different, and though they all set out from the same place and in roughly the same manner, the destination for many of them is different.

The tonal plan of the movement is as follows:

(1)		(2)		(3)	
E–d♯ ⎫		E–d♯ ⎫		E–E ⎫	
E–E ⎪	B(*Idée*)	E–E ⎪		E–E ⎭	
E–f♯ ⎬		E–f♯ ⎪			
E–E ⎭		E–g♯ ⎬	C(*Canto*)		
		E–A ⎪			
		E–B ⎭			

If this is translated into notes the relationship between it and the previously mentioned melodic line is immediately obvious.

(1)   Idée   (2)   Canto   (3)

These pilgrims are indeed made of melody. But, whatever their supposed geographical location, they sing with a decidedly French accent.

The great virtue of tonal movement by third and by step was its open-endedness, a quality which it shared with Berlioz' melodic methods, with his large-scale structures and with his general mental outlook. Apart from being the logical extension of the old diatonic practice, with which it could combine and which, therefore, it fulfilled rather than denied, it was sufficiently pliable to yield patterns of great complexity and of almost infinitely variable length which, nevertheless, possessed a natural musical coherence only to be described as organic.

A good example of all this is to be found in the over-all tonal organization of the first scene in *La Damnation de Faust*, where movement by third and by step is relieved by movement in fifths to form a complex whole which, in its general aspect, is an example of progressive tonality, moving from *D* to *G* majors.

The strength of this design—one could almost speak of its own inherent and expressive beauty—hardly needs underlining. Of itself it is an almost complete refutation of the common charge that Berlioz, whatever his other gifts, had little control of the principles of expressive musical form.

But in all of Berlioz' works there is no finer example of the new flexibility with which he endowed the known language than that to be discovered in the tonal organization of the *Angels' Chorus* in *L'Enfance du Christ*. Wholly expressive, enshrining one complete facet of the soul of Romantic sensibility, it nevertheless exhibits a Classical foundation which is startling in its conventionality. Whatever their spelling (*B:C♭–G♭:F♯–B*) the focal points of this chorus describe that conventional movement from tonic to dominant tonalities which we have seen to underlay so many of his extended movements and works. Here, however, in this truly angelic chorus, Berlioz makes no reference to 'sonata' structure. Within the bounds of this framework Berlioz' personal procedures are given full play. Nothing epitomizes more clearly than this chorus, with its tonal shifts of step and third embedded in an over-all modulation of a fifth, the true nature of his musical style and language.

Lento: B–d♯–e–C–D♭–D–f–G♭–C♭
Allegretto: G♭–D♭–G♭
Lento: F♯–A–B♭–B (for the rest of the movement)

As an extreme example of the tonal complexity made possible by Berlioz' expanded musical grammar we can take the *Course à*

l'Abîme from *La Damnation de Faust*. As one would expect, it is in pieces such as this—Romantic horror pieces, perhaps his most famed though by no means his most common type—that Berlioz brings all his resources into play, creating a tonal cauldron which never goes off the boil. In a subtle and symbolic way, two tonal usages are opposed to one another in this movement. Whilst Faust and Mephistopheles are caught up in a fast-moving whirlwind of key changes, the chorus of kneeling Christian women remains within the relatively calm *ambiance* of the tonic key, *c* minor. Throughout both the orchestral part has an almost Baroque figuration and rhythmic persistence, lending itself to innumerable symbolic interpretations as well as giving the whole an irresistible momentum and a coherent frame. Within the span of 128 bars (tempo direction *Allegro*) almost forty successive and definable changes of tonality are involved. But the nearer we approach to *Pandemonium* the more ambiguous and difficult to secure do the tonal areas become. There is a noticeable reliance upon the tritone in this approach to Hell, upon that peculiarly effective solvent of the 'fixities and definites' of tonal feeling and upon its handmaidens, the diminished triad and similar seventh. Of the twenty-four possible keys (old-style major and minor) only six are not involved—some of these last being rather surprising omissions. These are *C,G,A* and *B♭* majors, and *c♯* and *g♯* minors. Even in some of the appearances of those that are present, lack of the tonic chord gives them a subtlety of involvement which is truly Romantic. A good example of this is to be found in the passage from bars 67–70 inclusive, where *a* minor and *A♭* major are implied through the presence of either their dominant sevenths or ninths, or their diminished sevenths alone.

Thus, in the *Course à l'Abîme*, every degree save one of the chromatic scale is involved as a tonal centre, however transiently.

For the sake of clarity and convenience only, the movement may be divided into seven sections.

1	Bars 1– 19:	Faust
2	20– 42:	Chorus
3	43– 46:	Faust and Mephistopheles
4	47– 53:	Chorus
5	54– 66:	Orchestra
6	67– 89:	Faust and Mephistopheles
7	90–128:	Faust and Mephistopheles

If a tonal plan of the movement is drawn up the following pattern results.

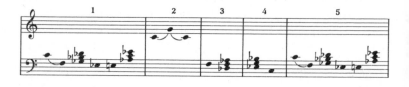

(In the above example all chords are minor unless otherwise stated. ⌣ signifies the tritone)

Several interesting facts emerge from a consideration of this pattern. In the first place, a considerable degree of overt formal cohesion is given to the first five sections by the exact repetition in section five of bars 2–14 from the opening section. In the second place, and less obvious perhaps, is the structural significance of the tonal shift *eb–e–Ab*, which occurs not only in section 1 (bars 10–14) and in section 5 (bars 62–66), but also at the very beginning of section 7 (bars 90–94), where its middle term *e* is translated into the major mode (*eb–E–Ab*). Thus, the greater part of the movement is informed by a kind of loose and subtle *ritornello* arrangement which, despite its lightness of touch, prevents the *Course à l'Abîme* from falling into structural chaos.

In the third place and perhaps of even greater interest to our study of Berlioz as a composer, is the re-arrangement in section 7 of the tonal groupings from section 1. What originally was

has become

and only one term (*Gb* in section 1), has suffered any change.

Finally, the tonal relationship between section 7 and the next part of the work, *Pandemonium*, is of great subtlety. The shift from *F* to *B* (either major or minor) which colours the last twenty-six bars of the *Course* is reflected in the first three bars of *Pandemonium*,

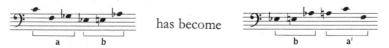

Has! Ir - i -mi-ra Ka- ra-bra - o!

and again at the end, when the whole movement subsides on to a *pianissimo* chord of *F* major, and the furies of Hell are quieted at last. Nor is this all, for the harmonization of the *Diff, diff merondor* section, pitched in the key of B major, is based initially on a scalic descent through a perfect fifth which includes the note *F* natural and the major chord upon it as one of its terms. Surely it is not just chance that the word carried by that chord is the name of *Mephisto* himself?

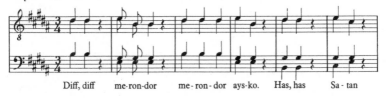

Diff, diff me-ron-dor me-ron-dor ays-ko. Has, has Sa - tan

Has, has   Bel-phe-gor, Has, has   Mel-phis-to, Has, has   kro-ix

When one recalls that Mephistopheles' first appearance is in the key of *B* major, shattering the calm of *F* major induced by the *Easter Hymn* and the subsequent ruminations of Faust, Berlioz' structural, symbolic and expressive intentions are clear. In his enhanced musical language the tritone, whether treated as a melodic interval or as a harmonic-cum-tonal relationship, is the point at which the soul of Man meets the Spirit of Darkness. Further evidence of this intention is supplied by the tonal plan of the *Choeur des Buveurs* in the same work, the extremities of whose first verse are a tritone apart,

$$c–E\flat–b\flat–D\flat–C–a–c$$

and also by the third line of *Brander's Song*, immediately following the chorus which, starting with the chord of *b* minor, cadences firmly in the key of *F*.

Mais   un beau jour le   pau - vre   dia - ble, Em -

- poi - son - né, sau - ta de - hors,

In this context one cannot help but recall the old medieval tag:

Mi contra Fa
Diabolus in Musica.

From a general as well as from a literal point of view, Berlioz' Romantic use of a Medieval concept to express the contemporary sensibility in music, is evidence of his creative historical sympathy. However fiercely he might rail against the superficial posturings of his fellow-composers, he extracted every possible ounce of value from the traditions and the practices of the past. And no matter how rebellious his music might *seem*—either to his contemporaries or to us—it was in essence a re-creation of tried and honoured principles and concepts, a revolution and not a rebellion.

As a final example of the expressive and symbolic use to which Berlioz put the tritone—that seed of self-destruction which tonality had always carried in its womb—let us examine the tonal plan of the *Dies Irae* section in the *Grande Messe des Morts*. The idea of a Day of Judgement, a day upon which, because of their own spiritual inadequacies, all things mortal shall once more be set in a state of primeval flux, is a truly terrible idea. Berlioz matched it with truly terrifying music: music in which threads of the ancient modality are inter-woven with strands of the modern tonality: music in which textures now contrapuntal, now polyphonic and now moving in massive blocks of homophony, are built into a vast architectural whole: music which is disciplined by the scholastic devices of canon and ground-bass: music contained within a tonal framework which moves inexorably across the interval of a tritone, from *a* minor to E♭ major. Just as in *Faust* the tritone was the point at which the human soul was touched by the hand of Evil, so in the *Dies Irae* it marks the point at which History is dissolved in Eternity.

a–b♭–d–E♭

The man who conceived all this and who fashioned it into a powerful artistic whole without at any point surrendering the integrity of his musical sense and expressive powers to the fashionable demands of Romantic theatricality, is a man to be respected by musicians and theologians both.

So much for the main features of Berlioz' most favoured tonal changes.

How were they achieved?

In a word, traditionally—by the well-worn methods of segments of the circle of fifths, the change of mode, the continuous
line, and the note held in common between two or more chords. As
always Berlioz took conventional methods and re-fashioned them
for his own expressive purposes. As a result we shall find few if any
outrageous chords in his music—nothing, for instance, like those
chords in the last movement of Beethoven's Ninth Symphony of
which he so strongly disapproved in his essay on that work. What
we shall find, however, is a new way of arranging these devices, an
exploitation of their latent possibilities, both separately and in
combination; in other words a whole new grammar which, without changing any of the basic resources of the musical vocabulary,
provides the structures necessary to express thoughts hitherto
unconceived.

Extended and unalloyed segments of the famed circle of fifths
seem to have been his least favoured procedure. Perhaps they were
too hackneyed, too obvious, and displayed overmuch of the
mechanics of tonal argument for his individual taste. But, however that may be, when he does use such openly conventional
methods, he manages to cloak them within the folds of a very
personal clothing. The best example of this is surely that to be
found in the first movement of the *Symphonie fantastique*. In the
exposition section the main burden of the conventional move to
the dominant key is carried by a descent through seven fifths in
as many bars, creating the modulatory plan

Ab–Db–Gb (F♯)–b–e–a–D–G

The rapidity with which the dominant chord is achieved is remarkable, for the first six strides occupy no more than $3\frac{1}{2}$ bars. It
must be one of the fastest-moving quintal progressions in music.

Generally speaking, Berlioz preferred to vary his tonal procedures within the course of a single over-all modulatory passage. As we have seen this method could produce patterns of great complexity and pliability, reflecting the parallel complexity of human experience yet remaining musically logical and expressively coherent both in detail and in extension. Sometimes, however, he gave progression in fifths a peculiarly individual flavour such as we find in the following passage from *Le Corsaire*.

The music is moving towards the tonic key of *C* for the final statement of the main theme. Starting from the chord of *A* major, it falls through four consecutive intervals of a fifth to the chord of *F* major. Then, dropping a third to the chord of *d* minor, it begins to move upwards by compound steps, each leg of which is a fifth apart from its individual companion, but a semitone or tone below its counterpart in the next compound step. The effect is exuberantly colourful and throws the *C* major theme into high relief.

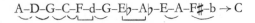

A–D–G–C–F–d–G–E♭–A♭–E–A–F♯–b → C

86

As for the transitional use to which Berlioz put a change of mode upon the same note, it is hardly surprising, in view of the modal ambivalence of his musical language, that this was a technique he very frequently used. If we do no more than review the majority of the examples quoted in this chapter so far, we shall find that most of them contain instances of this procedure. Its two great virtues were its poetry and its ease, qualities which had been recognized and acted upon for many years but never before pursued with such consistent intensity.

Such modal changes guide the shifts from F to $A\flat$ majors in the *Easter Hymn*, and from F to $D\flat$ majors in the vocal *scherzetto* from *Roméo et Juliette*. They smooth the transitions from D to F majors, C to $E\flat$ majors and from $E\flat$ to E majors in the *Dignare Domine* section of the *Te Deum*, and ease the shift from d minor to $f\sharp$ minor in the *Prologue* to *Roméo et Juliette*. They make logical the juxtapositioning of the chords of $B\flat$ and B majors at the opening of the *Oraison funèbre*, whilst its more extended use in *Le Spectre de la Rose* ($B\flat$–$D\flat$–$B\flat$) adds immeasurably to the poetic expressiveness of the song. Finally, it is a structurally essential part of the *Souvenirs* in the last movement of *Harold en Italie* (g–$f\sharp$$F\sharp$–$G$).

The truly Romantic subtlety with which this technique could be used is seen in the introductory section of *Carnaval romain* where, after the opening flourish in A major, a single note (E) is sustained on the horn. Until this is joined by a G natural on the clarinet this E retains its major feeling. But the clarinet alters the mode and so, with the minimum of fuss and the maximum of poetic effectiveness, prepares the way for the cor anglais tune in C major.

Of even greater economy of means, and of much deeper Romantic suggestion, is the single note which joins the end of Scene 15 to the *Invocation à la Nature* in *La Damnation de Faust*. A characteristic cadence in F major is succeeded after a pause by the sustained note *G♯*. If we go no further this is heard as an *A♭*, and we register a concluding change of mode from major to minor. But, if we proceed, the *c♯* minor chord which opens the *Invocation* entirely alters our view of it. Now we hear it as a preparatory dominant. In this ability to suggest the complex character and function of even a single note, Berlioz reveals something of the inner processes of Romanticism itself.

A final example is afforded by the connection between the *Oraison* and the *Apothèse* in the *Symphonie funèbre et triomphale*. Here, G major gives way to *g* minor when the chord of the former (on woodwind, horns and ophicleides) is followed immediately by a *B♭* roll on the timpani and, a bar later, an extended brass fanfare in the key of *B♭* major.

More examples could be quoted: but it is not my intention here to provide no more than a catalogue of Berlioz' musical habits. What is important for us to understand in this context is the expressive musical purpose which lies behind its so-frequent use.

From the fact that it is most often employed to guide modulations from a *major* tonic to the key on its *minor* third, either treated in its own right or as part of a larger modulatory scheme: or from the major tonic to the key on its flattened sixth degree equally permanent or transient: or again from a minor tonic to the key of its sharpened third or sixth degrees, we may deduce that Berlioz' prime intention was smoothness of transition, a smoothness which would allow both the bright colours and the pastel shades to fall across one another's path, and so leave no expressive tint un-evoked. It may come as something of a surprise to those who have read about Berlioz the man and heard of his reputation, but who have not really listened to, or studied, a great deal of his music, that smoothness, especially in the sense of linear elegance, was a quality which he valued highly in the fashioning of his works. But whether we consider his general relationship to the past, or undertake the more exacting task of examining the details of his craftsmanship, we cannot avoid the conclusion that both the attitude and the manner were organic and exceedingly logical. Berlioz evolved, he did not burst upon the musical scene. To treat him as a burster is to treat him superficially, to take the easy way out of an admittedly tough problem, to pose a scholastic solution to a Romantic challenge.

When we consider the next two modulatory procedures, the continuous line (diatonic, chromatic or mixed), and the common connecting note or notes, further evidence of Berlioz' concern for smoothness and elegance of logical connection appears at every turn.

Take, for example, the *Prologue* to *Roméo et Juliette*. Opening with a chord of F♯ major on the harp, the chorus leads the music to the brass chord of *d* minor: and it does so almost wholly by means of a descending chromatic bass line. The same technique informs the orchestral shift from *A* to *F* majors, and guides the choral move to *D* which follows immediately. And so it continues. Thus, a typically Berliozian tonal plan

b–dD–f♯–A–F–D–a–C–Ee

is made coherent and smooth-running by the essentially continuous lines which connect all of its members. The following short extract from the beginning of the movement in question illustrates the way in which the initial shift from *b–D* is accomplished.

Again, if we extract the bass line from the First Chorus part of the example quoted on page 69, we shall find that the downward tonal shift *e–d–C* is sustained by a falling chromatic line placed within, rather than below or above, the general texture.

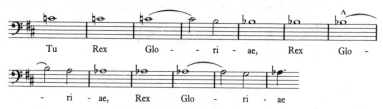

One of the most remarkable and far-reaching examples of the continuous line sustaining a whole segment of a work is to be found in the second verse of the *Easter Hymn* from *La Damnation de Faust*, and in the subsequent vocal recitative. In the Hymn a descending scale of *F* major extends across 28 bars, its first and fifth degrees (*F* and *C*) supporting 17 and 8 bars respectively, during which time they are seen from various points of harmonic view. *F* is treated as a root, third, fifth and seventh, whilst *C* appears as both a root and a fifth. All this occurs in the bass line.

In the following recitative, however, it is the vocal line which bears the linear emphasis. After an initial four bars it climbs upwards from *A* to *F* in a fully chromatic manner, which is resolved in the straightforward descent of the *F* major scale with which it closes and into which Mephistopheles, with tritonal significance, will shortly burst in the key of *B*.

Finally, as an example of the manner in which a continuous and almost wholly chromatic bass line could support a more conventional modulation from tonic to dominant, we may cite the transition passage from the exposition section of *Le Roi Lear*.

The use of commonly-held notes in adjacent chords to smooth out continuous modulatory passages which, otherwise, might be inappropriately violent in effect, is seen at its best in the *Angels' Chorus* which closes the first part of *L'Enfance du Christ*. We have already noted the essentially conventional nature of the tonal focus-points in this movement. What occurs between these points, however, is highly personal in both conception and execution. This chorus is almost the *locus classicus* of extended modulation by continuous line and common note. It is also a perfect example of that curious juxtapositioning of wholly unexceptionable chords which makes Berlioz' harmonic progressions so notorious, and which gives rise to those false ideas about the contents of his harmonic vocabulary. Although the whole chorus should be studied intently and at leisure, the following extract will be sufficient to demonstrate both the strength and the pliability of the techniques concerned, as well as their expressive power and logical nature.

Cases of such procedure are so common in Berlioz' works that it is unnecessary at this point to gather together a host of supporting examples. But it does have one particular use and extension which deserves a fuller consideration here. This is the pedal-point placed above, below or within a texture and which changes its tonal and harmonic significance several times within the course of a single passage or movement. Something of its pliability and expressiveness has already been noted in our comments upon the *Easter Hymn* on page 102. Whereas in previous styles it had been employed primarily as a climax-producing device, in Berlioz' hands it became one way in which the myriad fluctuations of Life itself could be reflected in musical sounds.

In this context something of a paradox, it makes secure that which essentially is unstable, gives rise to a host of conflicting sensations, peoples its musical world from within its own solitariness and lifts the veil which shades the face of Infinity. Perfectly suited to the Romantic sensibility, the pedal-point offers a thousand possible solutions to any single problem: and just as the tritone could symbolize the meeting-point of light and darkness, or of history and eternity, so the pedal-point can signify the immanence of poetry to prose and of magic to what the world proclaims reality. It is not surprising, therefore, that it appears most frequently in passages concerned either with the numinous or with the fantastic.

Take for example, the first five bars of *L'Invocation à Nature,* the remarkable method of whose introduction has already been noted. Beneath a sustained $C\sharp$ $(D\flat)$, a falling and continuous line supports a sequence of harmonies which, though in themselves straightforward, create in combination a startlingly unusual progression, and initiates a tonal shift from $c\sharp$ minor to $f\sharp$ minor.

Also from *La Damnation de Faust* comes our next example, the *Ballet des Sylphes*. The whole movement passes above a sustained pedal-point *D* whose tonal significance is now the root of *D* major or minor, now the fifth of *G* major or minor, and now the third in *B♭*.

As for its harmonic significance, this is even more varied, including membership of such chords as the diminished triad and augmented sixth, the tonic triad of *b* minor and the added sixth on the tonic note of *g* minor.

From the later part of the *Largo* introduction to the first movement of the *Symphonie fantastique* comes the next passage. For fourteen bars the sustained *A♭* (*G♯*) in the 'cellos and basses carries a variety of chords—*D♭*: *A♭*: *E*: *c♯*: *g♯*, and diminished seventh—which enables it to be seen as the tonic of *A♭* major or *g♯* minor, the fifth of *c♯* minor or *D♭* major, and the leading note of *a* minor. By what other musical technique could the idea of *Rêveries* be more effectively expressed?

A superior pedal-point of two notes—*E♭* and *D*—hovers over no less than twenty-three bars of the *Orgie* in *Harold en Italie*. It may be hard to classify the subject matter as numinous: but it certainly belongs to the world of personal fantasy! Beginning life as part of a dominant minor ninth in the key of *g* minor, it leads a chameleon-like existence above the chords of *B♭* major and the diminished triad in *g* minor: *b* minor and the first inversion of *g* minor: *c* minor and the diminished seventh in the same key. Finally, it falls to a single *D♭* note, and thus enables Berlioz to return to his tonic key of *g* minor by way of neapolitan harmony.

When we come to consider the adaptation of this technique in the remarkably moving *convoi funèbre* in *Roméo et Juliette,* technical description seems to verge upon the musically blasphemous, so perfectly is it done. The pedal-point is no longer entirely continuous, but made discrete, separated by passages of contrapuntal writing whose technical mastery should shame into silence all those commentaries upon Berlioz' supposed incompetence in this field. Within a simple tonal field (e–b–e–b–G–C–e–b–eE–E–B–E–b–Ee), the harmonic changes wrung upon the repeatedly chanted note *E*, choral and orchestral, include the augmented sixth, diminished and augmented triads, major and minor triads in varying positions, and the added sixth, as well as the dominant and diminished sevenths in several keys. By such means the conventional tonal framework and familiar contrapuntal texture is given a Romantic colouring and symbolic significance unequalled in the annals of expressive music.

Finally, in the *Offertorium* from the *Grande Messe des Morts,* the technique of the pedal-point achieves its apotheosis. Again, a relatively simple tonal field is filled with harmonic ambivalences surrounding a discrete, two-note ground which can be contracted or extended at will, and which can bear either a minor or a major colouring in the general tonalities of *D, F* and *A* and, the particular keys of *g* minor and *B♭* major. Something of its range and luminosity can be caught from the following quotation.

Rex____ glo - ri - ae!

Rex____ glo - ri - ae!

Rex____ glo - ri - ae!

If there is one single movement which contains within itself all, or almost all, of Berlioz' characteristic tonal procedures, that movement is the famous *Orgie* from *Harold en Italie*. Owing something in its general conception to the last movement of Beethoven's Ninth Symphony, it falls into two parts. In the first of these the themes of the previous movements are recalled on the solo viola in a kind of *ritornello* structure which moves from g minor to G major via F♯ major and f♯ minor, G major, e minor and C major.

Allegro frenetico	g	(ritornello)
Adagio: Souvenir de l'Introduction	g	
Allegro Tempo I	g	(ritornello)
L'istesso tempo: Souvenir de la Marche	F♯–f♯	(ritornello)
Souvenir de la Sérénade	G–e	(ritornello)
Souvenir du premier Allegro	C	
Tempo I : con fuoco	C–G	(ritornello)
Souvenir de l'Adagio	G	

In the second part, which follows upon the first without a break, the g minor material of the *ritornello* is combined with a new theme in B♭ major to form a kind of excised 'sonata' structure in which the repeated exposition is followed by a tonal excursion instead of a 'development'. This leads the music into G major, in which key the second theme is recapitulated by the full orchestra and after which a sudden theatrical *pianissimo* on the strings introduces a distant reminiscence of the Pilgrims' march. The way for the final peroration is cleared by the full orchestra working up to a perfect cadence in G major. The rest of the movement is taken up with this peroration, and elements of the *ritornello* reappear for the last time.

Although the focal key-areas of this part are wholly conventional (g–B♭:g–B♭–G), the complexity of the tonal patternings between them is second to none. The effect is more than kaleidoscopic.

1*st theme* (ritornello)   g–A♭–g–f♯

                        g–equivocal–g
                        a–equivocal–g

                        A♭–B♭–c
                          B♭–c–d
                        C–B♭–a–A♭–F
                        G–F–(E)–E♭–D–Cc–B♭ chord.
                                        │ chromatic scale over
                                          ↓ pedal *a*
                                      F chord.

         (ritornello)   B♭ + rising Gallic-type line to introduce
2*nd theme*   B♭ : interrupted cadence leads to V⁹ chord in g
                             tonal/harmonic change beneath superior
                             two-note pedal

                        chords B♭–dim 7 in g
                             b–$\frac{6}{3}$ of g
                             c–dim 7 in c: quickening repetitions
                                –dim 7 on B♭
                   A♭–g (Neapolitan extension)

                   ┌─────────────────────────────────────┐
                   g–B♭–c–B♭–g   1st time
                               interrupted by f♯ chord   │
                   –V⁹ in g

Complete repetition of above pattern but with alternative ending

            ┌──────────────────────────────────┐
   2nd time   g–B♭–g–V of g:
         │   B chord (V⁷ in e)
               e–G–a–b–C–d–e–c–dim 7 on G
                            dim 7 on F♯
                            V⁷ in G
                            dim 7 on F
                            V⁷ in G

2nd theme	G ending dim 7 on G
	C♯ note, strings: chromatic descent to B♮ note
	G (recall of *Marche* lontano)–b
	Build-up over pedal B (dom in E)
	G extended, decorated perfect cadence in G
Peroration	G–b (1st theme element i.e. ritornello element)–G

I shall not attempt to define the essentially equivocal details of
this section. But the following reduction will serve to show that,
whatever their individual peculiarities, they remain tonally con-
centric rather than eccentric. They confirm rather than deny the
tonic feeling by approaching it from all sides instead of directly.

The tendency to approach a specific tonality from a subsiduary key, to avoid stating the tonic chord (especially in root position) during the opening bars of a passage in a new key, or to imply a change of tonality by using no more than its secondary, equivocal or chromatically inflected chords, was a common practice with all the Romantic composers, and Berlioz was a master of this kind of tonal allusion. It was a powerful solvent of those fixed and definite formal outlines which they found so inhibiting. As long as it remained primarily harmonic it could be assimilated quite easily by existing structural schemes, as indeed it had been in many works of the preceding generation. But as soon as it became tonal it posed great difficulties, the chief of which was structural weakness. In all mature and extended tonal music structure ultimately depends upon the positive assertion of at least two main, and contrasting, tonalities. This is the minimum number. But that there is also an optimum number, and that this last depends upon the length and nature of the structure, is also true. To write music which involved numerous keys at different times, and which passed from one to the other by a system of coherent and logical connections was not only possible, but also necessary, if the whole art of tonal music was to remain relevant to the contemporary scene. But it demanded a creative, not an imitative approach to the problems of formal arrangement. Any great increase in the number of tonalities used required a parallel increase in the length and the sturdiness of the structures it informed. To attempt too much in too short a space of time and also within the framework of an essentially simple and well-worn scheme, was a sure guarantee of musical failure, however sympathetic to symbolic interpretation the resultant passage might be. Generally speaking, Berlioz avoided this pitfall with consummate success. *La Course à l'Abîme* is a first-rate example of this. But occasionally he fell into it head first, and the result was a movement such as the *Orgie*. However gratifying it may be to discover that the keys used in the 'sonata' section of the movement form, when arranged in alphabetical order, the complete ambimodal scale posited at the beginning of this chapter, one feels that such a profusion of tonalities within so short a space of time, moving at such a pace and within so well-established a framework, was a fundamental error of judgement on the composer's part. The simple schematic formula from the sonata age— minor tonic to relative major to tonic major—just cannot cope with nine other subsidiary tonalities, some of which appear in more than one mode, within so fast-moving and relatively short a movement. This profusion may indeed reflect that plentitude of human sensations which such a slice of life as that denoted by the title undoubtedly arouses. But as a musical proposition it is meaningless. Given time it might have worked: but on this scale, never. And this after all is the point, even in the Romantic Age, and especially in the case of Berlioz who was normally so astute in these matters. *La Course à l'Abîme* is successful because it uses instability only as a contrast with stability: because it expresses itself through the most pliable of all structural principles, *ritornello*: because it binds the whole together with a single and persistent rhythmic figure. Thus, although it fulfils all the Romantic requirements of symbolic and illustrative interpretation, it remains first and foremost a piece of music, an expressive artistic unity. This the *Orgie* does not. It puts programme, picture, mood or what you will before the notes, and the result is as uncharacteristic of the composer as it is unsatisfying to the ear and offensive to the aesthetic sense.

I cannot leave the subject of Berlioz' tonal procedures without at least mentioning his occasional passages of bi-tonality or polytonality. When they occur, which is not all that often, they are invariably the by-product of some polyphonic or contrapuntal texture. They are not consciously placed there primarily to create a startling dramatic effect, but are the organic and expressive outcome of an increasingly complex linear situation. Naturally, the instances vary in the degree of their tonal and structural complexity: but as indications of the two extremes of the possible gamut I quote the following examples. The first is from the *Dignare Domine* section of the *Te Deum,* and the second occupies a climactic position in the opening movement of the *Symphonie fantastique.*

The passage from the *Te Deum* welds together *G* major and *D* major above a pedal-point *D.* It is very simple: but the effect it produces is more complex, being deepened in subtlety by the passing references to *e* minor, *A* major and *b* minor which tint the orchestral part.

The climactic passage in the first movement of the *Symphonie fantastique* is of an entirely different order. It is my opinion—an opinion which seems to have been justified by our examination so far of his tonal procedures, and which will be further supported by our investigations of his harmonic practices in the next chapter—that Berlioz used organic tonality and developing harmony as the chief sustenances of his extended structures. In a very real way his works give tonal and harmonic evolution priority over thematic development. In this sense he certainly did take up music where Beethoven had left it; and in this sense, also, the whole tonal and harmonic system was of greater importance to his musical thought than it had been to that of any previous composer. Once more one is driven to acknowledge the peculiarly logical nature of Berlioz' personal musical revolution, and to understand why, things being as they were at that time, only a Frenchman could have accomplished it.

It is not possible to catch the full significance of this passage unless it is placed in its proper context. So, as a conclusion to this chapter, I shall attempt to trace its descent through the adventures of a single short chromatic line which makes its first appearance in the movement's *Largo* introduction. In all talk about music, words seem to overshadow the notes and sometimes even to defeat them. So, in this instance at least, the music shall be allowed to speak for itself, and the true order of priorities asserted at the last.

(i) **Largo** (2nd Violin)

(ii) **Allegro** (1st Violin)

(iii)

(iv)

(v)

[4]

Berlioz and Harmony

BERLIOZ' HARMONIC PROCEDURES HAVE COME IN FOR a good deal of harsh criticism during the past century and a half. Although some of his progressions remain musically unconvincing, the majority are wholly successful and, without exception, all are demonstrably logical. Any uneasiness which we may feel about this majority is due to our failure to appreciate the principles along which he worked—principles which allowed every single note in a melodic line to be treated individually, which sought to make the contour of every line in a progressing harmonic texture as elegant as possible, and which ultimately were governed by the concept of harmonic development and evolution. This last was an extension of a technique used by both Reicha and Beethoven —by the former in his *L'Art du Varier*, and by the latter in his sets of mature variations.

It is significant that Berlioz' harmonic practices should be so closely allied with both the art of variation (the most decorative and stylized of all musical techniques), and also with that of genuine melody. Whatever gift it may have had for tunes, the musical language of his time had little place for anything resembling true melody. This it had left behind, quite literally, in the Dark Ages. Its own natural speech was harmonic, and every melodic line—or better, tune—carried with it an implied and 'natural' bass. Although the individual details of each bass line were slightly variable, their general contours were circumscribed by accepted harmonic procedures and conditioned ultimately by well-tried tonal conventions. Thus, there existed a kind of Great Chain of Music in which tonality formed the topmost ring, and harmony, melody and bass-line the links immediately below. Now, by giving back to melody some of the freedom it had lacked since the far-off days of Gregorian chant, Berlioz somewhat relaxed the hold which traditional harmonic behaviour had upon it. Nor was this all, for the freedom he allowed his melodic lines as wholes was also enjoyed by each constituent note within them. Each was an entity in its own right, capable of being underlayed by any chord or number of chords relevant to it *per se*. Thus, the melody was less firmly linked with particular sets of known harmonic constructions and was free also to move through a correspondingly wider tonal field. The Great Chain was not broken at any point: but the hold which each link had upon the others was considerably relaxed and the diameter of the topmost ring very much enlarged.

As has been suggested in earlier chapters, this new freedom posed considerable musical problems and Berlioz' style was forced to become a compromise between convention and originality, a compromise which the traditionally-attuned critic was not always able to accept. In this sense the Berlioz style is the most comprehensive of all possible Romantic styles. On the one hand it offers an almost infinite variety of options: on the other hand it seeks to discipline them by a strict canon of behaviour. Symbolic, perhaps, of that conflict between the individual and society of which the Romantic sensibility was so conscious and by which it was so greatly stimulated, this inherent dichotomy within Berlioz' musical style cannot help but create a certain unease within the critical and academic breast. And unless its basic principles of action and particular methods of behaviour are studied carefully and sympathetically, they will often provoke mistrust.

Nothing shows more succinctly than the following excerpt from *Le Corsaire* the kind of tonal-cum-harmonic freedom enjoyed by Berlioz' musical lines. In it a recurrent and extendible figure in the violins is treated first as a member of a diminished seventh to tonic progression in the key of $D\flat$ major: then as the top of two consecutive diminished seventh harmonies: then as part of a diminished seventh to tonic progression in the key of G major: then to sustain a $\begin{smallmatrix}6\\4\end{smallmatrix}\begin{smallmatrix}5\\3\end{smallmatrix}$ to tonic move in the key of e minor: then as constituents of a similar progression in G major: and finally, after taking the music into D major, it ends as the surface of a conventional cadential phrase in the key of G major. When one sees that all this occupies no more than the space of thirteen bars (tempo *Allegro assai*) something of the kaleidoscopic effect produced by Berlioz' comprehensive treatment of individual notes can be guessed, and the strain to which he subjects his lines appreciated.

In such an expressive and wide-ranging language a strict canon of logical behaviour becomes an artistic necessity.

The principle of harmonic development is essential to the whole Berlioz style. Being one of his most original and least appreciated traits, it accounts for much of the misunderstanding that has surrounded his work. Rarely do melodies occur but once in the course of a movement or work, and almost never in their repetitions do they retain unaltered the harmonic dress in which they first appeared. Always this progressive harmonic variation serves an expressive as well as a technical purpose, carrying the music towards some emotional and sonorous climax and recreating rather than just filling out the particular structure it informs. Thus, and almost of necessity, it follows that the first statement of a theme, especially if it forms part of a 'symphonic' whole, will be accompanied by relatively simple harmonic relationships in a simple tonal field, and that sometimes these will be so lightly sketched as to seem almost non-existent. It also helps to explain the artistic necessity of devices such as *idée fixe*, or of formal principles such as *ritornello*, and to account for the large amount of melodic repetition which occurs throughout his extended works. The apparent incompetences of harmonic placement which accompany so many of his melodic lines at the outset of a work should never be heard or criticized as though they existed *in vacuo*. They must be seen as the first steps in a comprehensive and organic harmonic scheme which will not be completed, nor make any real sense, until the whole work or movement has run its course. They are indeed crude: but only in the proper sense of the word—as yet unformed and raw. It is present crudity for a coming end, artistic, sensitive, expressive, purposive and acutely intelligent. This last seems to bring us to the heart of Berlioz' own problem. It may be that he was too intelligent, or too clever, for the good of his own musical reputation. Perhaps he saw too many possible solutions to every technical problem and was not sufficiently selective or cold-hearted in these matters to choose only the musically most probable or appropriate. He may even have been attempting to do with music more than music could do—at least at that time. But whatever may be the final truth in all these matters, one thing remains absolutely certain—regardless of the programmes and literary associations heaped upon his music, either by himself upon occasions or by others throughout the century which has elapsed since his death, he never surrendered the autonomy of expressive music to outside influences. To expressive problems he propounded musical solutions, and though we are free to question their success, we can never doubt their integrity.

As in all other aspects of his compositional methods, the concept of organic reharmonization is open-ended and almost infinitely variable: whilst its ability to symbolize the subtlest fluctuations of the human spirit makes it peculiarly attractive to the Romantic sensibility. In the following extracts from Marguerite's *Romance* in Part Four of *La Damnation de Faust*, the process is seen at its clearest and most effective. Four times the same melodic pattern occurs at various points in the movement, twice in the orchestra and twice in the vocal line. In the orchestral appearances the harmonies are identical, moving from dominant to tonic in B♭ major and then from dominant to tonic in g minor. But in its vocal manifestations the underlying harmonic progression is each time different—in the first case moving from a $^6_4$ dominant chord in B♭ major to a diminished seventh on the note C♯, and then to a dominant seventh to tonic progression in g minor: in the second case, moving from a first inversion diminished triad on the note D through a similar position of the chord of d minor to a root position of E♭ major, which changes into a diminished seventh chord on the held note E♭, and closing with a dominant seventh to tonic sequence in the key of *g* minor. When one sees the order in which these varied harmonizations are arranged—Orchestral: Vocal 1: Orchestral: Vocal 2—the expressive intention of cumulative development and eventual climax becomes absolutely clear. Nothing could be simpler: nothing could be more effective. Nothing could have greater musical autonomy: yet nothing could possess greater expressive force.

In its sequence of tension, relaxation and then still-greater tension, it not only anticipates the Hindemithian system as outlined in the *Craft of Musical Composition*, but also reflects, though in a different dimension, that sequence of tension and relaxation which was found to inform the characteristically Gallic melodic line discussed in Chapters Two and Three. There it was seen in its melodic and tonal-cum-structural guises. Now we see it working analogously in the field of evolving harmony. Something of the comprehensive unity of Berlioz' musical style can be caught from this trinity of functionings.

Within a smaller and more immediate framework, the following passage from *Le Corsaire*—a work which repays detailed study, for it contains many of Berlioz' most characteristic procedures—exhibits the same features and function.

One of the most impressive examples of the kind of formal coherence which reharmonization of even the simplest figure can engender, is to be heard in the second movement of the *Symphonie funèbre et triomphale*. It also illustrates Berlioz' inclination to harmonize from the top downwards rather than upwards from the bass, as well as his use of harmonic alteration in the service of comprehensive musical and expressive development.

The opening chords present a thrice-repeated falling semitone figure at two different pitches—*D* to *D♭*: *G* to *F♯*: *G* to *F♯*. As was noted previously, the tonal purpose at this point is to achieve the key of *e* minor.

Twenty-four bars later, when the tonal aim has changed to *E♭* major, this semitone figure—now between the notes *E♭* and *D*—is repeated three times without any change of pitch but with altered harmony beneath its second note at each repetition.

Finally, towards the end of the main section in *G* major, it re-appears in a pattern whose melodic arrangement is the reverse of that in the opening bars, changing the pitch on its last, instead of on its second, appearance.

There is a beauty about this design as a whole analogous to that which informs the melodic line of the *Prélude* to *Les Troyens à Carthage* and independent of the particular music in which it is clothed. Designs such as this throw a significant light upon the character of Berlioz' craftsmanship, illustrate the workings of that *inexplicable mechanism* of which he himself was so conscious and

help to clear away some of the mists of rhapsody which too often
have surrounded Romantic music generally.

On the level of psychological complexity, the myriad reactions
of the various individuals in the crowd, as well as the changing
temper of the innkeeper himself—an extremist might include also
the various characters of the wines concerned—are all reflected in
the varieties of harmonic treatment to which the repeated phrases
of his tonally-rising expostulations are submitted. In this quite
remarkable passage from *Benvenuto Cellini* harmonic evolution,
tonal development, musical progression and emotional complexity
are all conveyed at one and the same time by musical, and none but
musical means.

Reflecting similarly the complexity of feelings which fill the mind and heart of the solitary and love-lorn Romeo, this simple two-bar phrase in *F* major repeats itself four times in immediate succession, and with each repetition the harmonic character changes and develops.

In its turn, this passage and its later literal repetition is a tonal and harmonic development of the original statement, which appeared in the *Prologue* in the key of *D* major and where its harmony remained unaltered. Once more the structural implications of harmonic evolution—its ability to make long works coherent by repetition which is at the same time varied—are clear. Nor could there be any better demonstration than this of the fusion of feeling with exposition which was Berlioz' particular concern.

But perhaps the most remarkable of all Berlioz' reharmonizations is that which sustains the whole length, and determines the essential structure, of the *Tibi Omnes* section in the *Te Deum*. Here an eight times repeated four-bar phrase, repetitions full also of the subtlest melodic variation and assembled into three separated groups, is given a new harmonic and/or tonal significance with each appearance. Statements 1–3 all close with the tonic chord. But whereas the first also begins with this chord, the others do not. They move from dominant seventh to tonic, and from mediant to tonic, respectively.

The next group, comprising statements 4, 5 and 6, is more varied still. Number 4 begins with the mediant chord and ends with that of the submediant: number 5, though finally closing with the tonic chord, is imbued with the tonality of the supertonic since it begins on the dominant seventh of that key and spends no less than three-quarters of its time therein: whilst number 6 opens with what appears to be a diminished seventh on *a*, but which is really a chromatically decorated chord of the dominant minor ninth in first inversion, and whilst suggesting the supertonic tonality of its predecessor during its own course, concludes quite firmly at the last in the tonic key of *b* minor.

The third and last group presents the original melody, first in *E* major and then in *f♯* minor, the subdominant and dominant minor keys respectively.

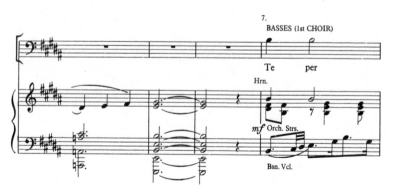

No verbal description, couched in semi-technical terms, can do proper justice to the subtlety of this remarkable movement, with its repetitive structure enframed within a prelude on the organ alone, and a reminiscent postlude divided between the organ and the strings. In itself it is almost a complete demonstration of that concept of expressive harmonic and even tonal evolution which informs Berlioz' individual musical language and which was perhaps his most original contribution to the art he both revered and loved. By developing it successfully he enabled a later generation of composers, and especially those of the Russian school, to come to terms with the structural problems imposed by the symphonic use of folk-song and its repetitive and diversified derivatives. It also substantiates part at least of Berlioz' claim to have been the true successor of Beethoven.

Berlioz' harmonic procedures are so rich and varied that to categorize them all in a clear and orderly fashion, leaving nothing to one side, seems virtually impossible. However, certain formal occasions and logical methods bring out all that is most characteristic of this aspect of his style, and some of these we shall consider now.

If there was one section of a structure which, more than any other, seems to have stimulated his harmonic imagination, that section was the peroration, coda and final cadence. Without ever losing its sense of basic tonal security, Romantic exuberance here creates a generally fast-moving, harmonic-cum-tonal kaleidoscope which consummates everything that has gone before. Something of its range and brilliance has been seen in the abstract of this particular section of the *Orgie* given at the end of the last chapter. Chords follow upon one another in the strangest juxtapositionings: keys flash past the ear with the colourful effect of Romantic lightning: and perfect cadences are continually frustrated by subsiduary clauses of sonorous rhapsody. If we begin our discussion of this subject with the final cadence we shall see in how many different ways, and from what a variety of harmonic directions, Berlioz was wont to approach his final chord. His distaste for the conventional Italianate close was summed up in his remarks about the conclusion of the second movement of Beethoven's Eighth Symphony—*I have never been able to explain to myself this comical wind-up.* Certainly, it sounds inappropriate to this day: and equally certain is it that few if any cadences in Berlioz' own music would sustain so obviously the text which, humorously, he attributes to the close of the Beethoven movement—*felicità.*

In the five Overtures which were discussed at the beginning of the last chapter the final cadences in each are all approached from different directions. Admittedly, some are more conventional than others: but all are slightly different.

Waverley	French sixth—dominant 7—tonic
Les Francs-juges	Diminished 7—tonic—dominant—tonic
Le Roi Lear	Mediant—dominant—tonic
Le Corsaire	Flattened submediant—flattened mediant— dominant 7—tonic
Benvenuto Cellini	Rising $^6_3$ chords—supertonic $^6_3$—dominant- tonic

The five movements of the *Symphonie fantastique* also exhibit a characteristic reluctance to close in the wholly conventional manner.

1. Extended plagal cadence using both modes of the subdominant chord
2. Mediant—submediant—dominant—tonic
3. Tonic minor (timps)—dominant note (strings and cor anglais)— first inversion and root of tonic
4. Tonic minor—tonic major
5. Mediant—added sixth on subdominant minor—first inversion of seventh chord on supertonic major—tonic—dominant—tonic.

Examples of this nature could be assembled almost *ad infinitum*. But in almost all of them we should find an emphasis placed upon the third and sixth degrees of the scale, either natural or flattened, which reflected the similar emphasis informing the tonal contours of at least part of the movements of works they closed. Equally, we should notice the frequent appearance of the chords of the diminished seventh and the augmented sixth (of whatever suppositious nationality): the noticeable if less frequent presence of Neapolitan harmony: a constant apposition of both modes of the tonic chord: a regular use of the plagal cadence, also involving both modes of the subdominant chord.

A small-scale example typical of the Berlioz peroration, coda and cadence is found in the overture *Carnaval romain*. Preceded by a plagal and a perfect cadence in the tonic key, the music descends through four consecutive steps of a fifth (*A–D–G–C–F*), of which the last member is in first inversion, and which is achieved at four times the speed of the others. Immediately after this the chord of *c♯* minor gives way to that of its major mode, and moves to the dominant chord by means of normal submediant harmony and a

French sixth on the flattened submediant. A chain of rising $^6_3$ chords takes us to the dominant seventh of the dominant, which introduces an extended perfect cadence in the tonic key of *A* major. The final cadence consists of the submediant and tonic chords presented above a sustained tonic pedal in the bass.

All these facts seem to me not only to support the contention that at heart Berlioz' musical language is based upon a semi-chromatic and ambimodal scale, but also that the tonal and har-monic complex which results from this is as concerned with the evolution of sonority as ever it is with more conventional thematic development. The reflection of large tonal contours in small-scale harmonic progressions, and the consummating exuber-ance of the perorations and more local climaxes, point to a true understanding of formal principles of the tonal and harmonic variety and fit in with his appreciation of the much larger problem concerning the whole deployment of time and space in composi-tion, musical or architectural, psychological or expressive.

Mention has been made above of the regular use of plagal cadences in Berlioz' music, and particular attention has been drawn to the variability of the mode of the subdominant chord in this progression. On the surface there is nothing unusual about this, since his language is essentially ambimodal as well as semi-chromatic. But also it signifies something more. Berlioz' overt use of ancient modality in movements such as the Overture to the second part of *L'Enfance du Christ* is well known, and its expressive purpose in such contexts is obvious. Nor does it require great imaginative effort on our part to appreciate the 'timeless' quality which imbues the ground of the *Dies Irae* for instance, and to acknowledge that some of this at least is due to his partial employ-ment of an ancient mode instead of a modern key. But it is less obvious, perhaps, that his frequent plagal cadences also grow from the same root, especially since so many of them involve *only* the minor chord of the subdominant. In a musical language as rich as that of Berlioz the subtle fertilization of his own brand of tonality by the more peculiar characteristics of old modality and in con-texts other than the liturgical or specifically 'sacred', seems not unlikely. Certain it is that, in his novel *Gambara,* Honoré de Balzac referred to the essentially religious nature of the plagal cadence: and certain it is, also, that there was a marked increase in the frequency with which this cadence was used during the nine-teenth century. It seems possible, therefore, that the Romantic awareness of the numinous quality inherent in all things found general expression in this old and hallowed formula. But, whereas with most composers the usage was based upon a somewhat diffuse and sentimental appreciation of the distant past, with Berlioz it grew from the vital roots of his intensely logical and expressive musical language.

However this may be, the ambimodal ground of Berlioz' language allowed him to use the flattened leading-note and the *dominant minor* chord also, for poetic reasons with the greatest of ease. An effective and well-known instance occurs at the final cadence of Faust's *Invocation à la Nature*, a movement which in its opening stages moves from *c♯* minor to *f♯* minor to *D♭* major—an extended i–iv–I plagal progression however its terms are spelt.

As a final comment on the frequent individuality of his cadential passages, nothing is more stimulating than the examination of the last *Amen*s in the *Requiem*. It was said in the second chapter, where the bass line of the present example was quoted, that many of Berlioz' melodic or semi-melodic lines were informed by a particular pattern which seemed to be peculiarly attractive to the Gallic sensibility. Subsequently, this line of thought was expanded in Chapter Three where the tonal contour of the *Marche des Pèlerins* was shown to have been guided by exactly the same pattern. Now, in Chapter Four we can see that the curious succession of harmonies with which the *Requiem* concludes is also dependent upon this pattern. Often they have been accounted as no more than the outcome of felicitous chance. But I think we have seen enough of Berlioz' methods of work to know that nothing in his music ever happens thus. Indeed, it is my firm conviction that most Romantic music is the product of careful and conscious manufacture on the various composers' parts, a process which had necessarily to be secretive in an age dedicated to 'inspiration': and that of all composers working along such lines, Hector Berlioz was by far the most mechanical, the most premeditative and, in the commonly accepted sense of the word, the least rapturously inspired of them all.

When one compares this sequence of chords with the sequence which opens the *Agnus Dei* section: when one sees that the successive roots of the latter make a pattern very similar to the former, but in reverse order: and when one compares both of these together with the corresponding incline and decline which frames the whole of the opening *Requiem et Kyrie* section, then one is amazed at the extent and depth of Berlioz' formal understanding and control, and overcome with admiration for the manner in which he uses harmony as an expressive tool in the service of a musical evolution which is at heart linear.

All Berlioz' sonorous curiosities, both tonal and harmonic, are the product of complex and extended linear activity: and the logic of any harmonic progression which strikes the ear as strange when considered vertically is explained immediately one examines the contours of the individual lines which sustain it.

During our discussion of Berlioz' tonal practices, attention was drawn to the use to which he put tied notes or notes held in common between successive chords, smoothing out harmonic juxtapositions which otherwise might have been too violent for the immediate context and guiding transitions between unusual tonal sequences. Particularly did we mention the *Angels' Chorus* from *L'Enfance du Christ*, and the opening bars of *L'Invocation à la Nature* from *La Damnation de Faust*. In doing this it was impossible to avoid impinging upon the preserves of this present chapter. But this has one advantage for it removes the necessity of covering the ground again. However, for the sake of shapeliness and order two further examples, each with different expressive intentions, are given here. The first concerns the illumination of a particular word by a simple harmonic change: the second is taken up with an extended introduction to a complete orchestral movement.

The first is the setting of the word *amour* in the *Prologue* to *Roméo et Juliette*. Here, the chords of *d* minor and C♯ major are placed side by side, and the progression kept in place by the common note in the tenor and alto line, which changes its harmonic significance, though not its spelling, from F to E♯. The expressive result is a sonorous radiance exactly matching the quality of Romeo's love for Juliette and of Shakespeare's portrayal of it.

son a - mour

The second example is the passage of thirty bars which introduces *Un Bal* in the *Symphonie fantastique*. Here, by means of a succession of completely ordinary chords, each with a note or notes in common with its immediate predecessor and successor, and the whole moving over a chromatically ascending bass line, Berlioz creates a passage of burgeoning excitement and gradually brightening colour which gives an entirely new expressive dimension to the simple apposition of mode (*a–A*), which essentially it is.

174

As well as using quintal progression to accomplish or assist in accomplishing tonal change, Berlioz employed it as a means of achieving harmonic colour or expressive climax, sometimes with remarkable effectiveness. The most obvious example of this is to be found in the Overture *Les Francs-juges*. Because it is wholly diatonic it has a slightly old-fashioned ring, a feeling accentuated by the neo-Corellian climbing figures in the violin lines. What individuality it does possess, however, is due largely to its upward direction. Generally speaking, the composers of the Romantic period used extended movement upward in fifths at least as frequently as its opposite, the more common practice of previous generations. It is possible that, consciously or unconsciously, this frequently indulged inversion of established and academic practice was one musical equivalent of the general Romantic tendency to turn the known world upside down.

F–C–g–d–a–e–B♭–F–C–g–d

In this context it is significant to recall that the *Eroica* symphony contains a progression of rising fifths in its development section (*f–c–g–d–a–e*): and that this upward movement is exactly balanced by a descending progression (*d–g–c–f–b♭–E♭*). Nothing is more indicative of Beethoven's own unique and unclassifiable position. The rhythmic transformation of the theme in the second movement of the same work is another prophetic stroke, as indeed is the very idea of a funeral march in a symphony. These last two points go to support the contention that the Beethoven style is more frenchified than generally we are willing to admit, and helps to account for the slight but noticeable Gallic strain which informs the Romantic style in music as a whole. Beethoven took from the French tradition all that he could use, infused it with his own artistic character and then handed it on to European composers generally. Hence to some extent the 'Romanticism' of Beethoven, to which his successors paid so much attention and from which they drew so large a part of their inspiration.

As one would expect, Berlioz treated progression in fifths as personally as he did all other well-worn patterns of behaviour, sometimes achieving effects of harmonic colour and expressive tension which are startling in their vividness and impact. Such a case is found towards the close of the first movement in *Harold en Italie*, where not only is the general movement in an upwards direction, but also its steps form a sequence of alternating perfect and diminished fifths.

C♯–G♯–D–a–E♭–B♭

One of his most interesting adaptations of quintal sequence occurs in the recapitulation section of *Le Corsaire*. Short and effective despite its immediate repetition, it consists of no more than two consecutive steps, the first of a perfect fifth upwards (*C♯–G♯*) and the second of an augmented fifth in the opposite direction (*G♯–C*). The character of the sequence lies in the diminished seventh chords which are erected upon these notes, a chord whose essential ambiguity made it particularly attractive to all Romantic composers.

Berlioz exploited this chord of the diminished seventh almost to the limit of its possibilities. When grouped into a series the resultant sense of tonal ambiguity was open to every shade of poetic symbolism: and when used as part of a more precise grammatical construction, it could so dissolve the 'fixities and definites' of conventional tonal relationships that the most unusual juxtapositions became both logical and coherent. Now there is a paradox here which it is worthwhile to acknowledge at once. In the previous chapter it was suggested that Berlioz valued smoothness of transition between one *tonality* and another: and the care which he took over these transitions seems to support that suggestion. But in the details of these transitions—that is in the *harmonic* progressions he employed to achieve them—not everything is quite so smooth, despite its always undoubted logicality. Thus, there are occasions when either the unfamiliarity of the particular sequence involved, or the speed at which the transition is achieved, breeds a certain discomfort in the ear, and this must either be accepted on its own expressive terms or else rejected on the grounds of strict academic impropriety. Either way, acceptance or rejection tells us more about the listener than it does about the music, a common though not altogether desirable state of affairs in much so-called music criticism.

Of the former and more immediately poetic use of a series of diminished seventh chords, nothing is more characteristic than that found in the following excerpt from *Le Spectre de la rose*.

Such progressions are frequent in Berlioz' music where a sense of spiritual, bodily or factual disintegration is involved, either in the text of a vocal work or in the expressive intention of an orchestral piece.

When two such series are deployed in simultaneous contrary motion, the effect is more than doubled, especially if one group moves in steps of a semitone and the other in steps of a tone. This is the case in the two following examples, the first of which is from *Les Francs-juges* and the second from the *Prélude* to *Les Troyens à Carthage*.

It is easy to see how such a complex progression, using the whole-tone scale as one of its fundamental elements, prepared the way for the eventual dissolution of tonality itself. A composer who wrote this kind of thing made atonality not only possible, but also necessary. From the time of such passages onwards it became part of the logic of events.

Of its more precisely syntactical use (either singly or in pairs), examples are legion. It seems to have been Berlioz' habit to envisage any constituent note in the chord as a possible leading-note in a new key, or even as a root, third or fifth in the next chord. Such a view, though never explicitly stated by him, is consistent with his apparent attitude towards the individual notes of his melodic lines, each one of which could be seen from a variety of points of view. In the case of the diminished seventh chord this view gave him a greatly increased number of possible resolutions, all of them logical, yet each enshrining its own peculiar expressive colouring. In the search for the *genre instrumental expressif* what could be of greater value?

Another very well-established chord for which Berlioz found a personal use, was the augmented sixth. Apart from employing it frequently in the conventional manner, as a single member of a simple, climactic progression, he liked, in moments of expressive intensity, to create a series of such progressions. Each in itself was conventional: but taken as a whole and clothed in enharmonic spelling, they produced a startling musical effect. In the following quotation from the end of Faust's *Invocation à la Nature*, they make possible a characteristic and complex tonal change of a semitone down plus a tone up,

C–b–c♯

and create an expressive climax of almost desperate power.

It is illuminating to compare this passage with a similar one which occurs earlier in the movement, Here, an equally complex tonal design of a semitone plus a tone is achieved by the same method. But in this case both tonal shifts are in an upward direction.

B♭–B–C♯

Moreover, the augmented sixth chords which introduce them are in positions other than the root, and two instead of three in number. Once more we see at work the evolutionary attitude towards tonality and harmony so characteristic of Berlioz' style, now refined to the ultimate degree, and using different positions of the same chord, as well as increasing frequency of its appearance, as members of the great organic and expressive musical progression.

Finally, in common with all other composers of the Romantic period, Berlioz made frequent use of Neapolitan harmony, generally in cadential passages and in perorations, and the two examples given here may stand as representative of them all. The first is taken from the last twelve bars of *Le Roi Lear*, and uses the Neapolitan sixth primarily for its colouring.

The second example is an expansion of the traditional cadence, and occurs in the last movement of *Harold en Italie*.

Berlioz' harmonic method was both his most original and his most considerable contribution to nineteenth-century music. Giving his own work a sound of rich individuality, it provided for his successors a grammar sufficiently pliable and open-ended to cope with simple tunes, folk or art, *fixe* or otherwise, repetitive or repeated, in a symphonic or near-symphonic context. It is ironic that this should have been inspired initially by lines more nearly approaching true melody than had any others since the time of Bach, and that the real sustenance of his strange harmonic progressions should have been an apparently deep concern for the smoothness of the lines in every constituent part. At heart, therefore, Berlioz' harmony is polyphonic: and just as the apparent atonality of the climactic passage in the first movement of the *Symphonie fantastique* had been a by-product of complex linear activity, so were the 'incorrect' progressions which appeared on nearly every page of his scores. Examine any one of these and you will discover that it is held together by a pattern of linear behaviour as considered and as logical as that of the strictest fugue.

Perhaps the most remarkable fact about Berlioz' harmony, however, is the plain ordinariness of its vocabulary, which nowhere exceeded the common parlance of his time and which, like it, derived ultimately from a passionate concern with opera. All the Romantic shudders with which his music abounds materialize through chords as well-worn as the minor ninth, the diminished seventh and the augmented sixth. If they sound fresh this is due either to their curious juxtapositioning one after the other, or else to their own unwonted positions *per se*. Berlioz was a master of the inversion and knew exactly the different emotional colourings of the various positions of the same chord, and his power of manipulation in this respect exceeded that of almost any other composer before or since. His frequent avoidance of root positions at focal points, and his corresponding refusal to acknowledge the force of the 'natural' bass and the predetermined close, were the seeds from which grew his power of expressive musical extension. The myriad solutions he propounded to familiar musical problems revealed an intensity of creative intelligence, and a depth of expressive imagination, shared by few men of his time, let alone musicians. His was one of the most acute minds of the nineteenth century: and whatever profession he had chosen to follow he was bound in the end to have achieved unusual results. His geometrical approach to composition preserved the integrity of music as an *art* in an age that ran very close to seeing it solely as a means of *self-expression*. Whatever Berlioz' music expressed, it was certainly not this, though the depth of his personal reaction to sound ensured that whilst divorced from sentimentality it was never detached from sentiment. In this context it is illuminating to recall some remarks which he made in the course of a criticism of Meyerbeer's *Les Huguenots*, published in the *Journal des Débats* on November 10th, 1836.

Amateurs sometimes question the purpose of the long course of study to which composers submit themselves, the point of what they call the musician's science: it is to produce marvellous works of *art* [his italics] like this, not with the childish aim of astonishing, but in order to arouse feelings in which pleasure and admiration are interfused: it is to accomplish finally and effortlessly the often arduous tasks which are imposed upon him by certain situations, certain *données dramatiques,* in which the happiest contrasts crowd together but which, in incompetent hands, would produce nothing but disorder and chaos.

It is in the harmonic field and particularly in his realization of the organic potential of harmonic evolution, that Berlioz' claim to have taken up music where Beethoven left it can most easily be vindicated. This was a much more fundamental thing than the overt imitation of formal schemes, the kind of activity in which most other men indulged and which led to so many curious choral symphonies and passages of inflated keyboard bluster or orchestral rhodomontade. At heart Berlioz may have been a traditionalist in the widest sense of the word: but he was never just imitative; and his ability to see the nature of music's inherent problems where others saw nothing but the shape of another man's answers indicates the quality of mind which informed what was perhaps the period's most remarkable musical achievement.

[5]

Conclusion: the Berlioz Style

THOUGH DEEPLY EXPRESSIVE, THE BERLIOZ STYLE IS A premeditated style in which nothing happens by accident and in which very little, on the surface at least, is spontaneous. The carefully designed melodies, the planned tonal changes and the logically contrived harmonic progressions together amount almost to a nineteenth-century doctrine of affections. What is said fuses wholly with the manner of its saying, and every pattern occupies the place it does for a specific expressive or symbolic purpose. It was precisely because of this systematic arrangement that Berlioz was able to discipline his native exuberance, restrain the fire which burnt within him and realize the expressive potential of his musical conceptions. Thus his art is a stylized art, much less 'Romantic' than the common view would have it to be, and typical of the deepest instincts of French thought.

For this reason most of his works, and particularly those massive creations which he himself referred to as architectural, have a detached, static and sculptured quality, perfect embodiments of the Gallic sense of plastic values. He was able to stand back from his own work, to appraise and to criticize it, to see *ma musique* always in the light of *la musique* and to secure the integrity of art from the hysterical incursions of self-expression. Bad performances of his works he described as those in which *the principal features of my figures are either altered or defaced*, terms which consciously or not reveal his own deep sense of plastic shapeliness and contour. These works hang between heaven and earth, the vibrancy of their equilibrium sustained equally by technical control and spiritual vehemence. Because of this detachment they are essentially liturgical and oracular, and a great deal more powerful as a result. These are rare qualities indeed and not with composers alone. As Berlioz knew to his cost, every performer and particularly every conductor, needs a sense of plastic beauty commensurate with his own to make them succeed. In his own words *they ought to feel as I do*, and this *feeling* is as much literal and tactile as ever it is metaphorical or emotional. The combination of *extreme precision* and *irresistible verve*, or the fusion of *regulated vehemence* with *dreamy tenderness* is not a common one, even amongst good musicians; and it is this demand for the rare—on the part of scholars, critics and audiences as well as on that of performers and conductors—which is responsible for much of the common misunderstanding of his music.

The Berlioz style is also a prose style, asymmetrical, continuous, open-ended and dramatic, naturally adapted to immensities of space and time yet constantly aware of every least refinement of detail. It is a rhythmic art which has outgrown the need for metre: a poetic art beyond the bounds of verse. His large open structures are capable of a comprehensiveness beyond the formal schemes of most men because each constituent musical cell encloses a whole universe of emotional designs. Like Shakespeare he is able to match comedy with tragedy, oppose sorrow to joy and inspire a public gesture with personal reaction all within one work, even within one section or within a single melodic line, without ever losing control of its over-all design and expressive purpose. His relationship to literature therefore is one of analogy rather than one of illustration. Confusion over this point is resolved immediately the music is examined *per se*, for it is always self-supporting if never self-sufficient. In an age entranced by the versified simplicities of folk song and folk poetry, titivated by the symmetrical sensualities of Italian arias and hypnotized by the regular incantations of a Scribe; at a time when there was both an emotional tendency and a financial inducement to speak to the lowest common denominator in the easiest possible way, Berlioz' music was bound to remain eccentric. Whilst other men acknowledged poetry as *the mother tongue of the human race* or *the common gift of all mankind*—German statements both—or agreed with Framèry that *by its very nature music is symmetrical*, adapting its techniques to the requirements of their particular media, Berlioz addressed a different audience. Both his music and his critical writings were aimed at that small group of musically sensitive and artistically cultivated persons who possessed the right kind of ears to hear them. This is an old-fashioned aim, with an exclusive and eighteenth-century ring, having more in common, perhaps, with the principles which inspired the events of 1789 than with those which erupted in 1830 or 1848. In an age devoted to the ideals of bourgeois sentimentality he had the courage to espouse the cause of aristocratic refinement, and, appropriately enough, the price he paid was reckoned in both hard cash and insulting words.

The Berlioz style is also essentially polyphonic and linear, able to dispense with the stricter contrapuntal schemes of the musical schoolmen which were the product of harmony rather than of line, and emphasizing the principles of linear development which they had sacrificed to the demands of chordal progression. This is seen most clearly in those passages of supposed atonality which occur at climactic points in works like the first movement of the *Symphonie fantastique*, and even more in his ability to draw all the basic elements of music itself into the contrapuntal web. In Berlioz' polyphonic textures melodic line may be counterpointed by rhythmic pattern or harmonic progression, and even his phrasings, dynamics and instrumentation create an extended texture rather than a vertical pattern.

The Berlioz style is also an evolutionary style which adds to the past by using it rather than by overturning it. His methods of melodic creation—the careful manipulation of expressive linear formulae—were as old as melody itself, and in this respect his roots lie in the ninth century and beyond, stretching their tendrils into the ancient Mediterranean littoral which he understood so well and which was never so finely portrayed as in *Les Troyens*, nor ever more aptly turned to a contemporary theme than in the *Symphonie funèbre et triomphale*. Thus, by a paradox as strange as any that one may encounter in a lifetime, the orderliness and logic of his method was of the very essence of Romanticism. That feeling for the reality and the texture of the past, at which so many of his contemporaries played and over which so many of them lost their heads rather than their hearts, was the basic inspiration of his character.

In his works therefore Berlioz not only showed his contemporaries the way in which music could most profitably develop in the future, but also he summed up everything which it had already achieved in the past. In as much as he could, he restored to melody the freedom of movement and design which it had lost centuries before. His tonal changes exploited all the possibilities that Beethoven had envisaged without in any way destroying the fundamentals of the natural tonal system. His harmonic progressions showed how the grammar of music could be refashioned for Romantic ends by exploiting to the full established aesthetic criteria and all this without having to increase its basic vocabulary by so much as one new chord. This was a tremendous *technical* achievement, something for which he has not received the credit due to him and something which matches his expressive and sonorous achievement step for step.

Index of Names

Aristotle, 43
Bach, J. S., 193
Barbier, Auguste, 41
Balzac, Honoré de, 4, 5, 168
Beethoven, 17, 19, 21, 23, 44, 46, 162,
   194, 198
   Symphony no. 1, 64
          no. 3, 183
          no. 7, 6, 73
          no. 8, 9, 162
          no. 9, 3, 12, 80
   variations, 146
Bennet, 41
Butterfield, H., 14
Byron, 24, 31
Chateaubriand, 3
Cherubini, 9, 11, 13, 25
Framèry, N. E. de, 197
Gautier, Théophile, 5
Genet, Jean, 3
Gluck, 7, 11, 38
Gossec, 6
Gounod, 13
Grétry, 6
Haydn, 2

Hindemith, 150
La Fontaine, 3
Lesueur, Jean François, 7, 13, 19, 22
Liszt, 2, 16
Lucas, F. L., 17
Méhul, 6, 14
Messiaen, 2
Meyerbeer, 5, 6, 9, 194
Napoleon, 7
Rameau, 2, 11, 12, 32
Reicha, 9–11, 12, 14, 21, 46, 51, 146
Reti, Rudolf, 27
Rousseau, Jean-Jacques, 3
Saint-Saens, 13
Schlegel, A. W., 3, 41
Schubert, 64
Schumann, 3, 40
Scribe, Eugène, 197
Sénancour, Étienne Pivert de, 12
Shakespeare, 6, 41, 43, 171, 197
Strauss, Richard, 2
Toreinx, F. R. de., 46
Vinci, Leonardo da, 14
Wagner, 3

WORKS BY BERLIOZ REFERRED TO AND QUOTED FROM

Benvenuto Cellini, 4, 40, 153–5
   Act Two, 64–5
   Overture, 44, 46, 163
   Prière, 6, 7, 33–4, 43
Carnaval romain, 44, 46, 47, 49, 96,
   163–7
Le Corsaire, 34–6, 38, 40, 42, 43, 44, 46,
   55, 84–95, 147–8, 151, 186
La Damnation de Faust, 39, 55–6
   Ballet des Sylphes, 112
   Brander's song, 68, 70–2, 78–9
   Choeur des Buveurs, 78
   Course à l'abîme, 45, 74–7, 133

Easter Hymn, 47–8, 67, 78, 96, 102,
   111
Invocation, 96–7, 111–12, 169, 171,
   191–2
Opening to Part 1, 49–51
Opening to Part 2, 61
Pandemonium, 77–8
Romance, 31–2, 42, 43, 149
Scene 1, 71
L'Enfance du Christ, 4
   Angels' Chorus, 6, 12, 45, 61, 74,
   103–10, 171
   Opening, 54–5

Index